Measuring Effectiveness

LIBRARY
I.U P
Indiana, PA

HM
131
.M39
1981

Dan Baugher, *Editor*

NEW DIRECTIONS FOR PROGRAM EVALUATION
A Publication of the Evaluation Research Society
SCARVIA B. ANDERSON, *Editor-in-Chief*

Number 11, September 1981

Paperback sourcebooks in
The Jossey-Bass Higher Education and
Social and Behavioral Sciences Series

In Memory of
DR. CAROLYN WILK
I.U.P. Professor 1974-

D1384498

Jossey-Bass Inc., Publishers
San Francisco • Washington • London

Measuring Effectiveness
Number 11, September 1981
   Dan Baugher, *Editor*

New Directions for Program Evaluation Series
A Publication of the Evaluation Research Society
Scarvia B. Anderson, *Editor-in-Chief*

Copyright © 1981 by Jossey-Bass Inc., Publishers
                        and
                        Jossey-Bass Limited

Copyright under International, Pan American, and Universal
Copyright Conventions. All rights reserved. No part of
this issue may be reproduced in any form—except for brief
quotation (not to exceed 500 words) in a review or professional
work—without permission in writing from the publishers.

New Directions for Program Evaluation (publication number
USPS 449-050) is published quarterly by Jossey-Bass Inc.,
Publishers, and is sponsored by the Evaluation Research Society.
Second-class postage rates paid at San Francisco, California,
and at additional mailing offices.

Correspondence:
Subscriptions, single-issue orders, change of address notices,
undelivered copies, and other correspondence should be sent to
New Directions Subscriptions, Jossey-Bass Inc., Publishers,
433 California Street, San Francisco, California 94104.

Editorial correspondence should be sent to the Editor-in-Chief,
Scarvia B. Anderson, Educational Testing Service, 250 Piedmont
Avenue, Suite 2020, Atlanta, Georgia 30308.

Library of Congress Catalogue Card Number LC 80-84298

International Standard Serial Number ISSN 0164-7989

International Standard Book Number ISBN 87589-858-0

Cover art by Willi Baum

Manufactured in the United States of America

Ordering Information

The paperback sourcebooks listed below are published quarterly and can be ordered either by subscription or as single copies.

Subscriptions cost $30.00 per year for institutions, agencies, and libraries. Individuals can subscribe at the special rate of $18.00 per year *if payment is by personal check.* (Note that the full rate of $30.00 applies if payment is by institutional check, even if the subscription is designated for an individual.) Standing orders are accepted.

Single copies are available at $6.95 when payment accompanies order, and *all single-copy orders under $25.00 must include payment.* (California, Washington, D.C., New Jersey, and New York residents please include appropriate sales tax.) For billed orders, cost per copy is $6.95 plus postage and handling. (Prices subject to change without notice.)

To ensure correct and prompt delivery, all orders must give either the *name of an individual* or an *official purchase order number.* Please submit your order as follows:

Subscriptions: specify series and subscription year.
Single Copies: specify sourcebook code and issue number (such as, IR8).

Mail orders for United States and Possessions, Latin America, Canada, Japan, Australia, and New Zealand to:
Jossey-Bass Inc., Publishers
433 California Street
San Francisco, California 94104

Mail orders for all other parts of the world to:
Jossey-Bass Limited
28 Banner Street
London EC1Y 8QE

New Directions for Program Evaluation Series
Scarvia B. Anderson, *Editor-in-Chief*

Contents

Editor's Notes

The evaluation and assessment of program and institutional effectiveness is becoming a widespread activity, and, as a result, the field of evaluation is evolving into a "professionalized" discipline (Freeman and Solomon, 1979). Although such issues as experimental design and program approaches generate considerable debate (Conner and Dickman, 1979), it seems clear that the need for specialists with broad interests in measuring effectiveness is growing. Ironically, however, the field of evaluation does not really constitute a new set of activities (Anderson, 1978). Questions of measurement and assessment have existed for some time; the basic question of "How can I measure effectiveness in this situation?" has plagued managers, teachers, and researchers for years. The prevailing concern with test validity and accounting techniques documents our continuing interest in analyzing effectiveness.

Yet, the measurement of effectiveness is not as simple as it may appear on the surface. Such measurement requires a broad understanding of social values and human nature as well as skill in the application of statistically complex measurement techniques. Values, as well as politics, influence the kind of answers given to the initial questions asked by those developing a measurement strategy: "What constitutes effectiveness in this situation?" "How will the information obtained be used?" Answering these questions is often the most difficult problem evaluators face. Key administrators frequently have no definite idea of what kind of evaluation is wanted (Heilman, 1980). As a result, the measurement specialist must be as adept in answering the broad questions of "what" and "what for" as he or she is in answering the question of "how."

This volume focuses on the difficulties inherent in measuring effectiveness and offers some potential solutions to these problems for a diverse set of measurement situations. Chapters focus on the assessment of effectiveness for organizational activities, psychopharmacological research, and education.

Organizational Activities

Measuring the effectiveness of organizations and their activities has posed many problems for both researchers and managers (Connolly and Deutsch, 1980). Organizations are complex systems: effectiveness in one organizational activity or department does not necessarily imply effectiveness in other areas. Furthermore, the measurement of worker effectiveness is as critical to understanding organizational effectiveness as the measurement of departmental and general functions.

The first three chapters in this volume are directly concerned with the measurement of organizational, departmental, and worker effectiveness. In the first chapter, Cameron suggests that it is impossible for evaluators to measure organizational effectiveness from all relevant points of view. He poses six critical questions that investigators should answer in order to clarify what kind of effectiveness is being assessed in their studies. Next, Varanelli takes the derived goal model of organizational effectiveness (Price, 1972; Steers, 1977) and uses it to assess university computing centers. Because these centers have limited and concrete outputs, he finds this approach useful for highlighting areas of computer center performance and for developing operational and perceptual measures of centralized delivery system success. In the third chapter, Bulgaro and Frucher examine the problems associated with developing and using a performance appraisal system that links public sector employee effectiveness to salary increments. Not the least of the problems they describe is the difficulty of translating broad public policy into specific tasks on which managers and employees can be evaluated. The most important problem, however, is that of motivation. Public sector managers must be convinced that accurate performance evaluations will actually help them meet their departmental goals. Only then will the appraisals be completed in an appropriate manner.

Psychopharmacological Research

Clinical investigators, the drug industry, regulatory agencies, and the general public are all concerned with safe and effective medications. Nevertheless, each of these groups has different notions of what constitutes proof of efficacy and satisfactory methodology. The fact that clinical evaluation is not an exact science, especially in the case of mental illness, makes it difficult to obtain exact answers to questions of efficacy (Levine, Schiele, and Bouthilet, 1971).

In the fourth chapter, Wittenborn and Kelsey recognize the importance and difficulties inherent in drug research and provide information regarding acceptable clinical study of drug efficacy. They briefly outline "The International Guidelines for the Clinical Investigation of Psychotropic Drugs" (Wittenborn, 1977) and the procedural standards of the Food and Drug Administration (FDA). Taken together, these constitute the most up-to-date standards for the measurement of efficacy in this field. Information about the kinds of problems emerging from FDA audits of drug research is also provided. From their analysis, we are left to question whether a heavy emphasis on measures of procedural effectiveness might not foster ineffectiveness in other areas (for example, increasing cost of drugs for the consumer or slow development of new drugs).

Educational Activities

The development and education of workers and students is an extremely important activity in our society. Yet literature on educational and training effectiveness lacks conceptual clarity and is often marred by the use of unsound methodological approaches (Mathis, 1980). In order for an educational program to be successful, the goals of the program must be outlined clearly before the program is begun. The assessment of the program's efficacy must also be determined through the use of sound measurement tools and design strategies.

Chapters Five, Six, and Seven discuss questions of educational goals and effectiveness measurement. The fifth chapter provides an in-depth consideration of the barriers to the assessment of training efficacy. In this chapter, I review training programs for the "disadvantaged" and offer the conclusion that poorly conceptualized goals and weak studies of training efficacy limit the success of these programs considerably. This chapter also includes an outline of some requirements for administering a successful remedial training program. In the sixth chapter, Gormly considers the broader enterprise of education and directs our attention to the goals of our school systems. He suggests that direct behavioral observation through videotaping can help uncover the "actual" goals of our schools. He also discusses the "preferred" goals of an educational system. From his perspective, a comprehensive assessment of school systems must include ongoing assessments of students' social and personal skills as well as their academic achievement. In the seventh chapter Kippel presents a measurement model for assessing the academic achievement of individual schools within a school system. In general, his model suggests that certain errors in prediction may be systematic and not random. He then uses regression procedures to determine which schools are exceptional and whether there are any consistent differences between "overachieving" schools and "underachieving" schools.

The divergent perspectives of the chapter authors clearly indicate that there is no single model of effectiveness applicable to all situations. In the last chapter, however, I attempt to outline points of general agreement. For the most part, the authors agree that multiple measurements of efficacy are essential in almost every situation. Multiple measurements make for a balanced perspective and allow the values of most interested parties to be taken into consideration. In addition, those involved in the measurement of effectiveness must operate with an understanding of human nature if their work is to be of any operational use. Most individuals react strongly to an evaluation of their effectiveness. Some see it as a personal attack. Because of this fact, effectiveness measurement must be future oriented and avoid concentrating on past problems or faults. Otherwise, administrative resistance will seriously jeopardize the measurement program.

Dan Baugher
Editor

References

Anderson, S. B. "Editor's Notes: The Expanding Role of Program Evaluation." In S. B. Anderson and C. D. Coles (Eds.), *New Directions for Program Evaluation: Exploring Purposes and Dimensions*, no. 1. San Francisco: Jossey-Bass, 1978.

Conner, R. F., and Dickman, F. B. "The Professionalization of Evaluative Research: Conflict as a Sign of Health." *Evaluation and Program Planning*, 1979, 2, 103–109.

Connolly, T., and Deutsch, S. J. "Performance Measurement: Some Conceptual Issues." *Evaluation and Program Planning*, 1980, 3, 35–43.

Freeman, H. E., and Solomon, M. A. "The Next Decade in Evaluation Research." *Evaluation and Program Planning*, 1979, 2, 255–262.

Heilman, J. G. "Paradigmatic Choices in Evaluation Methodology." *Evaluation Review*, 1980, 4, 693–712.

Levine, J. R., Schiele, B. C., and Bouthilet, L. *Principles and Problems in Establishing the Efficacy of Psychotropic Agents*. Washington, D.C.: Public Health Service, U.S. Government Printing Office, 1971.

Mathis, C. B. "Evaluating the Effectiveness of Teaching." In E. H. Loveland (Ed.), *New Directions for Program Evaluation: Measuring the Hard-to-Measure*, no. 6. San Francisco: Jossey-Bass, 1980.

Price, J. L. *Handbook of Organizational Measures*. Lexington, Mass.: Heath, 1972.

Steers, R. M. *Organizational Effectiveness: A Behavioral View*. Santa Monica, Calif.: Goodyear, 1977.

Wittenborn, J. R. "Guidelines for Clinical Trials of Psychotropic Drugs." *Pharmakopsychiatrie Neuro-Psychopharmakologie*, 1977, 4, 205–264.

Dan Baugher is an associate professor in the Lubin Schools of Business Administration of management, Pace University, New York City. He is interested in the prediction of socially relevant criteria, such as employee effectiveness, through an examination of individual differences. He has worked as a consultant on problems of measurement and prediction for AT&T and Hardee's Food Systems, Inc.

*Effectiveness is an elusive concept that can be
approached through several models, none of which is
appropriate in all circumstances.*

The Enigma of Organizational Effectiveness

Kim Cameron

The underlying goal of most research on organizations is to improve their
effectiveness. It is ironic, therefore, that no concrete definition of organizational effectiveness has yet emerged and that there is general lack of agreement as to the proper approach for assessing effectiveness (Cameron, 1978;
Goodman and Pennings, 1977; Steers, 1977). Debates about which definition is best continue in the literature (Molnar and Rogers, 1976; Price,
1972), and some writers have become so discouraged with the ambiguity of
the concept of organizational effectiveness that they suggest dropping it
from the academic vernacular altogether (Goodman, 1979; Hannan and
Freeman, 1977).

Some of the chapters in this volume focus on *program* effectiveness,
which is different from *organizational* effectiveness. Program effectiveness,
refers to success in performing a program—a specific set of behaviors, tasks,
and purposes defined by the designers or initiators of the program. Most
organizations, however, comprise multiple, contradictory, and often
ambiguously specified programs, which are defined by a broad array of
constituencies. Therefore, adopting a single indicator of organizational
effectiveness—such as profit—may serve to measure success in one program
but does not address the other multiple programs operating simultaneously in the organization.

D. Baugher (Ed.). *New Directions for Program Evaluation: Measuring Effectiveness*, no. 11.
San Francisco: Jossey-Bass, September 1981

Another term that is often confused with organizational effectiveness is *efficiency*. Organizational efficiency is generally understood to be the ratio of organizational inputs to outputs, or the amount of resources expended in the production of an organizational output. Little controversy exists either about this definition or about how to measure efficiency. Such is not the case with effectiveness. No simple ratio exists that specifies successful organizational performance. Effectiveness resides in the values and judgments of individuals; efficiency is not a matter of individual judgments. It is clear, therefore, that efficiency and effectiveness are not the same—that an organization may be efficient but not effective and vice versa—and that the relationship between efficiency and effectiveness may be either positive or negative.

In this chapter, some of the confusions attending the definition and assessment of organizational effectiveness are discussed, and the four most prominent approaches to the assessment of effectiveness are reviewed. The conditions under which each of these approaches is most appropriate are pointed out as are some of the weaknesses in each approach. The chapter concludes with an explanation of some critical questions. These questions serve as a framework for the assessment of organizational effectiveness and provide evaluators with guidelines in choosing what to assess and how to assess it.

Problems in Defining Organizational Effectiveness

There are at least three reasons why organizational effectiveness has remained an ambiguous and ill-defined concept. First, there are several conceptualizations of what an organization is and of how organizations differ from one another. For example, organizations have been viewed as rational entities in pursuit of goals (Perrow, 1970), as coalitions reacting (or proacting) to strategic constituencies (Pfeffer and Salancik, 1978), as individual need-meeting cooperatives (Keeley, 1978), as meaning-producing systems (Weick, 1979), as information-processing systems (Galbraith, 1975), and so on. As the definition of what an organization is changes, so does the definition of what an *effective* organization is.

With the hope of identifying salient effectiveness criteria, several authors have attempted to develop typologies of organizations or to determine what major characteristics are typical of different types of organizations (for example, Haas and others, 1966; Hall and others, 1967). Unfortunately, these efforts have failed. What this failure means for organizational effectiveness is that the search for indicators of effectiveness usually begins anew in each organizational evaluation. No standard set of criteria is available with which to evaluate effectiveness in organizations because no standard organization exists.

Table 1. Model Used to Define and Assess Organizational Effectiveness

Model	Definition	When Useful
	An Organization is Effective to the extent that. . .	
Goal Model	it accomplishes its stated goals.	Goals are clear, consensual, measurable
System-Resource Model	it acquires needed resources.	Clear connection between inputs and outputs
Internal Process Model	it has an absence of internal strain, smooth internal functioning.	Clear connection between processes and primary task
Strategic-Constituencies Model	all strategic constituencies are at least minimally satisfied.	Constituencies have powerful influence; the organization reacts

for example, is especially useful when organizational goals are clear, consensual, and measurable. That is, when desired end states can be identified and progress toward them monitored, then the goal model is appropriate for assessing effectiveness (Price, 1972).

The system-resource model is most useful when there is a clear connection between resources received by the organization and the products of the organization. For example, an organization that simply gathers resources and stores them is not effective. Similarly, obtaining resources not associated with the primary task of the organization simply increases "organizational fat" and contributes to inefficiency.

The process model is most appropriate when the internal processes of an organization are closely associated with what the organization produces or with its primary task. In other words, the process model is most appropriate when the outcomes of an organization are clearly linked to its internal processes and practices or to the smooth functioning of the organization's technology. A smooth communication flow on matters that are irrelevant to the tasks of the organization, for example, is not indicative of organizational effectiveness.

The strategic-constituencies approach is most appropriate when constituencies have powerful influence on what the organization does or when an organization's actions are largely reactive to strategic constituency demands. The mission or the domain of some organizations is mandated by external special interest groups; by contrast, other organizations are more proactive and autonomous in their activities. Similarly, some organizations exist in an environment where certain constituencies clearly are more powerful than others, whereas other organizations have no clear powerful constituency. In the former, the strategic-constituencies model would be a useful approach. In the latter, the model would not be effective.

There may be some circumstances in which any or all of these approaches may be appropriate for assessing effectiveness. None of these models, however, is appropriate in all circumstances and with all types of organizations. For example, one problem with the goal model is that it does not credit organizations with effectiveness in areas that do not coincide with their goals. In the 1960s, NASA's mandated goal was to reach the moon. During this time NASA was also very effective in producing useful consumer goods, an area in which no goals existed. It was only after men landed on the moon, however, that NASA's past contributions to consumer products were noted.

Another problem with the goal approach is that an organization can be ineffective even when it accomplishes its goals if the goals are too low, misplaced, or inadvertently harmful. For example, the Nestle Company, whose explicit goal was to provide nutritional aid to infants in Third World nations became so effective at replacing mothers' milk with baby formula that they are currently being accused of perpetrating malnutrition and starvation in underdeveloped countries.

The system-resource approach also is not universally applicable in evaluating effectiveness. For example, an organization can be effective even when it does not possess a competitive advantage in the marketplace or when it does not obtain the most desirable resources. For example, the coach of Alcorn State, the undefeated 1978–79 Division 2 NCAA basketball champions, bragged after Alcorn's victory that his team was composed of second-stringers. All the best players went to more prestigious and better-known schools, he claimed, and Alcorn State simply wasn't as competitive in recruiting as some of the opposing schools.

Conversely, an organization may be ineffective even when acquiring optimal resources and while being highly competitive in the marketplace. Several Swiss organizations, for example, became the most highly effective watchmaking firms in the world because of the excellence of their jeweled, hand-crafted watches. The microcircuit and digital revolution caught them so resource rich in this one market, however, that they found it almost impossible to switch domains. Their effectiveness is now very low in the new industry that manufactures lower-priced digital watches.

Exceptions can also be found to the applicability of the process approach, which defines organizational effectiveness in terms of internal organizational processes. For example, an organization may be judged highly effective even when its internal "health" is low (that is, when communication is poor, strife and conflict are present, and members are not highly integrated). A classic example is the strife-ridden New York Yankees, world champions in 1977 and 1978.

Economists frequently equate internal efficiency with organizational health, and effective organizations are thought to be those that are most efficient (that produce the least waste) or whose internal processes are the smoothest. Yet long-term adaptation and innovation are often enhanced by conflict and the presence of organizational slack (unused resources). Inefficiency sometimes produces effectiveness.

Conversely, organizations may be ineffective even when internal health is high or when the organization's processes are good. For example, Janis (1971) portrays President John Kennedy's cabinet as a highly cohesive, smoothly functioning group of decision makers. It was just these characteristics, however, that produced a "groupthink" phenomenon. The power of groupthink was felt in the decision to invade the Bay of Pigs. The group made a decision, later judged to be highly ineffective, that most cabinet members would not have made by themselves.

The applicability of the strategic-constituencies approach to evaluating effectiveness is also limited. Organizations can be rated as effective even though they ignore strategic constituencies or perform in contradiction to their demands. For example, in the 1930s Swarthmore college ignored the wishes of its students, alumni, and trustees by courting an elitist image. The now famous "Swarthmore Saga" by Frank Aydelotte proves that effectiveness can be developed in the face of strong resistance from organizational constituencies (Clark, 1970).

What these examples point out is that no single approach to the evaluation of effectiveness is appropriate in all circumstances or for all organizational types. Organizations may be judged to be ineffective even when meeting the criteria of each approach, or they may be judged to be effective even when not meeting the criteria.

Furthermore, as was suggested earlier, because of increasing turbulence in the external environment, more and more organizations are becoming characterized as loosely coupled systems or as organized anarchies. Cohen and March (1974), Weick (1976), and others have suggested that such organizations become typified by (1) ill-defined, complex, changing, and contradictory goals; (2) unclear connections between organizational means (technologies and internal processes) and organizational ends (outputs), with more than one technology producing the same end; (3) weak feedback loops with little or no feedback occurring from output to input, or feed-forward occurring from input to output; (4) different organizational parts, loosely connected to other parts, responding only to a limited set of environmental elements; and (5) widely differing criteria of success operating simultaneously in the organization. Other characteristics may also be enumerated, but these five illustrate why none of the four general approaches to effectiveness is appropriate in such organizations. The goal model requires identifiable, specific, measurable goals, but organized anarchies are purposely vague regarding goals in order to respond to a wide variety of demands and expectations. The organizations discussed elsewhere in this book are good examples. Schools, mental health facilities, and service organizations purposely espouse broad, nonspecific goals. Overspecificity of goals can be severely restricting to such organizations. The system-resource approach is also inappropriate because no clear causal connection exists between organizational inputs and outputs. For example, the budgets (inputs) of many government bureaus are based on the previous year's expenditures, not on services provided or evidence of effective production of outputs. The process model is not useful because internal processes have an ambiguous relationship to organizational outcomes. There is no evidence that the processes occurring inside the organization lead directly to a desired output. For example, there is no adequate empirical evidence that school courses produce educated individuals (Astin, 1977). Finally, because loosely coupled organizations are structured as they are precisely to reduce the influence of external constituencies on the organization and to serve as a buffer against environmental encroachment, the strategic-constituencies model also appears to be an inappropriate approach.

The enigma of organizational effectiveness, therefore, is that a consensual definition of the concept and a consistent approach to its assessment are limited by the nature of modern organizations. The major approaches to organizational effectiveness are altogether inappropriate in certain types of organizations, some definitions of effectiveness may be applicable in some circumstances and not in others, and the continuing research on organizational effectiveness seems only to add to the fragmentation and variety of the field.

Suggestions for Assessing Organizational Effectiveness

One reason for the lack of theoretical progress regarding organizational effectiveness is that organizations have many different ways in which to be effective, and they may be both effective and ineffective at the same time depending on the aspect of the organization (or the program) being considered. Attempts to assess overall organizational effectiveness ignore this variety. In my own work on the assessment of organizational effectiveness, I have argued that certain critical decisions must be made that limit assessments of effectiveness to a specific organizational referent. That is, by specifying the critical choices required in each assessment of effectiveness, a framework is provided that both guides the evaluator and achieves comparable results across different organizations. Comparability among studies is a result of classifying each evaluation in terms of the critical choices made.

The six critical decisions follow:

1. What domain of activity is the focus of the evaluation? Most organizations operate in a variety of domains. My own research shows, for example, that organizations differ significantly in the domains in which they are most effective. Effectiveness in one domain frequently mitigates against effectiveness in another domain (Cameron, 1981). The importance and relevance of particular domains of activity also change as organizations progress through their life cycles. Research on the developmental stages of organizations shows not only that different organizations emphasize and succeed in different domain(s), but that over time any single organization may change the domain(s) that it emphasizes (Cameron and Whetten, in press; Quinn and Cameron, 1980). An important decision to make when evaluating the effectiveness of organizations is the selection of the domain(s) of activity to be evaluated. Focusing on an outdated or inappropriate domain not only prevents accurate assessments of effectiveness but may also have negative consequences for the organization itself. For example, what is evaluated and measured is generally viewed as important in the organization, even though it may not be current.

2. *Whose perspective, or which constituency's point of view, is being considered?* Evaluations of effectiveness always reflect the values of some major constituency. That is, the criteria selected for any evaluation are derived from one particular point of view or perspective. Increased organizational effectiveness from one constituency's perspective may result in lowered effectiveness from another constituency's perspective.

Organizations seldom if ever satisfy all strategic constituencies, and certain constituency's viewpoints are more influential than others. Consequently, one way to evaluate the effectiveness of organizations is to select indicators of effectiveness that reflect the interests of the most powerful constituency in the selected domain.

However, highly effective organizations may not satisfy *any* constituency completely; they may satisfy incompletely various constituencies in multiple domains. Assessments from only one point of view would miss that diversity.

The selection of indicators of effectiveness to satisfy one powerful constituency, or the selection of more general indicators should be a conscious trade-off. What appears to be mediocre effectiveness from the standpoint of one constituency may really be high effectiveness when multiple perspectives are assessed.

3. *What level of analysis is being used?* This third critical question refers to the level of aggregation used in evaluating effectiveness. There are at least three broad levels to consider when evaluating an organization— effectiveness of individuals, effectiveness of groups or subunits in the organization, and effectiveness of the overall organization.

Effectiveness on each of these three levels of analysis may be compatible. However, effectiveness on one level may also mitigate against effectiveness on another level. Research on the developmental stages of organizations suggests that the importance of different levels of analysis changes as the organization develops (Cameron and Whetten, in press). Research by Hannan and Freeman (1977) shows that failure in organizations is frequently the result of focusing on the wrong level of analysis (that is, a level where the important behavior does not take place). Therefore, care should be taken to select an appropriate level of analysis, depending on the domain and constituency, despite the fact that some levels are more difficult to assess than others.

4. What time frame is being employed? The time frame employed in evaluations of effectiveness is important because effectiveness over the long run frequently is incompatible with effectiveness in the short run. For example, organizational slack leading to adaptability is necessary for long-term effectiveness, yet it is inconsistent with efficiency of operations, a frequently used short-term criterion of effectiveness.

A study of the United States tobacco industry, for example, found distinct differences among the relative effectiveness of six tobacco firms depending on whether long- or short-term criteria were used. Some firms were effective in the long run but not in the short run and vice versa (Miles and Cameron, 1977).

The choice of the time frame is important because organizations may trade off short-term effectiveness in order to guarantee long-term effectiveness. It is not unusual, for example, for a firm to keep profit margins low in the short run in order to increase market share or to increase sales in the long run. Organizations may also emphasize short-term effectiveness without considering long-term effectiveness.

5. What data are to be used in the evaluation? Another choice faced by evaluators of organizational effectiveness is whether to use as indicators information collected by the organization and stored in official documents or whether to rely on perceptions obtained from members of organizational constituencies. The choice is between objective data (organizational records) or subjective, perceptual data (interviews or questionnaire responses). Objective data have the advantage of being quantifiable, potentially less biased than individual perceptions, and representative of the official organizational position. However, objective data frequently are gathered only on "official" effectiveness criteria. The official focus may make the data rather narrow in scope. In addition, official data often relate to criteria of organizational effectiveness that do not have readily apparent connections to the organization's primary task (Cameron, 1978). The advantage of subjective or perceptual data is that a broader set of criteria of effectiveness can be assessed from a wider variety of perspectives. The disadvantages, however, are that bias, dishonesty, or lack of information on the part of respondents may hinder the reliability and validity of the data.

The selection of data by which to measure effectiveness is important because an organization may be judged effective on the basis of subjective perceptions while objective data may indicate that the organization is ineffective. Or, reversing the argument, objective data may indicate organizational effectiveness while perceptual data may indicate ineffectiveness (as found by Varanelli in the next chapter).

     6. What referent is being employed in the evaluation? Once indicators of effectiveness have been selected for evaluating an organization, one can use a variety of referents against which to judge those indicators. One alternative is to compare the performance of two different organizations against the same set of indicators (comparative evaluation). The question is, "Are we more effective than our competitor?" A second alternative is to select a standard or an ideal performance (for example, Likert's (1967) system 4 characteristics) and then compare the organization's performance against the standard (normative evaluation). Here the question is, "How are we doing relative to a theoretical ideal?" A third alternative is to compare organizational performance on the indicators against the stated goals of the organization (goal-centered evaluation). "Did we reach our stated goals?" A fourth alternative is to compare an organizaton's performance on the indicators against its own past performance on the same indicators (improvement evaluation). "Have we improved over the past year?" A fifth alternative is to evaluate an organization on the basis of the static characteristics it possesses, independent of its performance on certain indicators (trait evaluation). In this approach, desirable organizational characteristics are identified. The evaluation reflects the extent to which the organization possesses those characteristics. The relative advantages and disadvantages of these referents make them appropriate for certain types of organizations and certain circumstances and not for others, but space considerations do not permit an elaboration here. The point is that it is important for evaluations of organizational effectiveness to determine the referent against which to compare effectiveness indicators, since it is conceivable that one organization may be effective relative to one referent (for example, accomplishing its goals) but ineffective relative to another referent (for example, in comparison to major competitors).

Conclusion

     Organizational effectiveness has become an enigma. Its definition and assessment have produced more confusion than enlightenment. This confusion arises from the characteristics of many modern organizations and because of the limited applicability of the major models of effectiveness developed so far. The meaning of effectiveness in academic research is unclear because of the variety of referents used. Lacking of guidelines or models, practitioners frequently use effectiveness as a post hoc justification for what the organization already does well.

     Evaluators of organizational effectiveness will never measure all of the relevant aspects of effectiveness of an organization from all the relevant points of view. Therefore, it is imperative that evaluators make explicit

12

certain critical choices they make when measuring effectiveness. These choices reveal what is being measured and how effectiveness is being defined. In this way, not only will the focal organizations benefit from understanding more exactly the meaning of the evaluation, but research on organizational effectiveness will begin to become more comparable and cumulative.

References

Astin, A. W. *Four Critical Years: Effects of College on Beliefs, Attitudes, and Knowledge.* San Francisco: Jossey-Bass, 1977.

Cameron, K. "Assessing Organizational Effectiveness in Institutions of Higher Education." *Administrative Science Quarterly,* 1978, *23,* 604–632.

Cameron, K. "Domains of Organizational Effectiveness in Colleges and Universities." *Academy of Management Journal,* 1981, *24,* 25–47.

Cameron, K., and Whetten, D. A. "Perceptions of Organizational Effectiveness Across Organizational Life Cycles." *Administrative Science Quarterly,* in press.

Campbell, J. P. "On the Nature of Organizational Effectiveness." In P. S. Goodman and J. M. Pennings (Eds.), *New Perspectives on Organizational Effectiveness.* San Francisco: Jossey-Bass, 1977.

Clark, R. *The Distinctive College.* Chicago: Aldine, 1970.

Cohen, M. D., and March, J. G. *Leadership and Ambiguity.* New York: McGraw-Hill, 1974.

Connolly, T., Conlon, E. J., and Deutsch, S. J. "Organizational Effectiveness: A Multiple Constituency Approach." *Academy of Management Review,* 1980, *5,* 211–217.

Cyert, R. M., and March, J. G. *A Behavioral Theory of the Firm.* Englewood Cliffs, N.J.: Prentice-Hall, 1963.

Galbraith, J. *Organization Design: An Information Processing View.* Reading, Mass.: Addison-Wesley, 1975.

Goodman, P. S. "Organizational Effectiveness as a Decision Making Process." Paper presented at 39th annual meeting of the Academy of Management, Atlanta, Georgia, August 8, 1979.

Goodman, P. S., and Pennings, J. M. *New Perspectives on Organizational Effectiveness.* San Francisco: Jossey-Bass, 1977.

Haas, J. E., Hall, R. H., and Johnson, N. J. "Toward an Empirically Derived Taxonomy of Organizations." In R. V. Bowers (Ed.), *Studies on Behavior in Organizations.* Athens: University of Georgia Press, 1966.

Hall, R. H., Haas, J. E., and Johnson, N. J. "An Examination of the Blau-Scott and Etzioni Typologies." *Administrative Science Quarterly,* 1967, *12,* 120–121.

Hannan, M. T., and Freeman, J. H. "Obstacles to Comparative Studies." In P. S. Goodman and J. M. Pennings (Eds.), *New Perspectives in Organizational Effectiveness.* San Francisco: Jossey-Bass, 1977.

Janis, I. L. "Groupthink." *Psychology Today,* November 1971, pp. 43–44, 46, 74–76.

Keeley, M. "A Social Justice Approach to Organizational Evaluation." *Administrative Science Quarterly,* 1978, *22,* 272–292.

Likert, R. *The Human Organization.* New York: McGraw-Hill, 1967.

Miles, R. H., and Cameron, K. *Coffin Nails and Corporate Strategies.* Englewood Cliffs, N.J.: Prentice Hall, in press.

Molnar, J. J., and Rogers, D. C. "Organizational Effectiveness: An Empirical

Comparison of the Goal and System Resource Approaches." *Sociological Quarterly*, 1976, *17*, 401–413.

Perrow, C. *Organizational Analysis: A Sociological View*. Belmont, Calif. Wadsworth, 1970.

Pfeffer, J., and Salancik, G. *The External Control of Organizations*. New York: Harper & Row, 1978.

Price, J. "The Study of Organizational Effectiveness." *Sociological Quarterly*, 1972, *13*, 3–15.

Quinn, R. W., and Cameron, K. "Organizational Life Cycles and the Criteria of Effectiveness." Working Paper, School of Business, University of Wisconsin, 1980.

Steers, R. M. *Organizational Effectiveness: A Behavioral View*. Santa Monica, Calif.: Goodyear, 1977.

Weick, K. E. "Educational Organizations as Loosely Coupled Systems." *Administrative Science Quarterly*, 1976, *21*, 1–19.

Weick, K. E. *The Social Psychology of Organizing*. (2nd ed.) Reading, Mass.: Addison-Wesley, 1979.

Yuchtman, E., and Seashore, S. "A System Resource Approach to Organizational Effectiveness." *American Sociological Review*, 1967, *32*, 891–903.

Kim Cameron is director of organizational studies, National Center for Higher Education Management Systems and associate professor, Graduate School of Business, University of Colorado. His primary research interests center on the assessment of effectiveness in organizations, particularly in those referred to as loosely coupled systems or organized anarchies.

*The goal model is appropriate for evaluating
effectiveness in computing centers and, by extension,
other service organizations.*

Evaluating Effectiveness in Computing Centers

Andrew Varanelli, Jr.

In the previous chapter, Cameron suggests that there are four different approaches to assessing organizational effectiveness now in common use. This chapter describes proposed procedures for using one of these approaches, the derived goal model (Steers, 1977), to evaluate the effectiveness of a complex service organization, a university computing center. In addition, the results of this application for ten different university computing centers are discussed briefly.

Determining the Goals of University Computing Centers

In order to evaluate the degree of effectiveness of an organization from the derived goal approach, one must determine the state of affairs or goals that the organization wishes to realize (Etzioni, 1975). The derivation of these goals requires an assessment of the organization's actual activities and apparent intentions (Gross, 1969). For computing centers, these activities and intentions are generally limited and concrete. First, the units of production for computing centers are measurable outputs. They can be measured in volume, in time, and in cost. Second, most people using a computing center will tend to perceive its intentions and effectiveness in terms of these measurable, concrete outputs. As a result, analysis of

D. Baugher (Ed.). *New Directions for Program Evaluation: Measuring Effectiveness*, no. 11.
San Francisco: Jossey-Bass, September 1981

perceptual as well as concrete operational data can point toward the actual goals of a computing center as well as its effectiveness in meeting these goals. More important, a lack of agreement between perceptual and operational measures of effectiveness may point toward subtle, but important, problems in the center's selection of goals and goal achievement.

For the above reasons, both perceptual and operational data are used in this study to measure the effectiveness of computing centers. University computing centers are viewed as striving toward four possible goals: adaptiveness, production volume, production efficiency, and staff job satisfaction. These goals reflect the work of Hage (1965); many studies have shown that Hage's axiomatic variables are among the most important goals sought by organizations and therefore are useful for measuring organizational effectiveness (Steers, 1977). Indicators for these four goals, as achieved in computing centers, are shown in Table 1. According to Fleckenstein (1972), these indicators are appropriate for the measurement of computing center effectiveness as well as sources of role conflict for computing center directors.

Development of Instruments*

The instruments* used in this study were designed to assess the degree to which a university computing center is striving toward and accomplishing the four variables suggested by Hage (1965). Both concrete operational data and user perceptions of the center's goals and effectiveness were obtained. Since a university computing center generally serves two main user groups—administrative and academic users—Hage's variables were interpreted somewhat differently for these groups. Some of the items in the instruments were either taken directly or derived from earlier survey instruments measuring computer center financial and production operations (Ivey, 1972) and effectiveness (Fedrick, 1971; Fleckenstein, 1972). The remaining items were developed by the author. The instruments were discussed with experts in the area in order to validate the item content (Nunnally, 1967). These experts included the marketing and research groups of several computer hardware manufacturers, faculty members and administrators at universities not included in the study, and various faculty members in the Pace University Department of Computer and Information Science. Based on these discussions, some items were modified and four instruments were produced:

1. The Measure-of-Performance Instrument. This questionnaire was employed to conduct a structured interview with the computing center director at each of the universities studied. It measures academic and administrative operational performance at the computing center. A selec-

*All instruments may be obtained from the author.

Table 1. Computing Center Effectiveness
Measures Related to Hage's Variables

Hage's Axiomatic Variables	Computing Center Indicators
Adaptiveness	Flexibility, the adaptation of new programs and techniques in providing computing services to the campus.
Production Volume	The volume of reports, data, programs, and services rendered by the computing center.
Production Efficiency	The amount of production relative to the cost of operating the computing center.
Staff Job Satisfaction	The morale of the computing center staff.

tion of the items from this instrument are given below. Each is keyed to one or more of Hage's variables: adaptiveness, production volume, production efficiency, and staff job satisfaction.

1. Number of computer languages supported for academic purposes—an academic adaptiveness item.

2. Whether or not special purpose academic languages such as WHATFOR and PL/C are available—an academic adaptiveness item.

3. Whether or not an academic newsletter exists—an academic adaptiveness item.

4. Whether or not a user's manual exists—an academic and administrative adaptiveness item.

5. Number of computer languages supported for administrative purposes—an administrative adaptiveness item.

6. Number of administrative systems installed—an administrative production volume item.

7. Power of available academic input-output (I/O) devices—an academic production volume and adaptiveness item. The power of I/O devices was simply a figure of merit. For example, a 10 cycles per second (cps) teletype-like device was given a weight of one. A 30 cps unbuffered teletype-like device was given a weight of four on the basis that the user could transmit to the computer at the same speed as the 10 cps device, but the computer could transmit back to the user at three times the speed of the 10 cps device. All other I/O devices were rated on this basis. Ultimately, the power of academic input/output devices at the center was a weighted average of the number of devices multiplied by their send-receive figures of merit.

8. Distributions of available computing time between administrative and academic users—administrative and academic production volume and production efficiency items.

9. Academic Input-Output turnaround—an academic production volume item.

10. Academic turnaround divided by amount of money spent on academic processing—an academic efficiency item.

11. Administrative Input-Output turnaround—an administrative production volume item.

12. Administrative turnaround divided by amount of money spent on administrative processing—an administrative production efficiency item.

13. Rate of turnover for computing center staff–a staff job satisfaction item.

14. Relative merit of computing center staff salaries—a staff job satisfaction item. The merit of staff salaries was determined by comparing the distribution of staff salaries in various positions to published distributions of salaries for the industry.

2. The Staff-Perceived Operational Goal Instrument. This questionnaire measures the staff's perception of the computing center's goals in terms of Hage's variables as well as their perception of the computing center's effectiveness in meeting these goals. The first section of this questionnaire consists of a ranking procedure that deals with the *computing goals* of the institution's center. Administrators were asked to rank the following list of common goals for university computing centers. These goals may be related to three of Hage's variables: adaptiveness, production volume, and production efficiency.

1. To improve the computational, statistical, and data manipulative capabilities of the faculty, staff, and students of the institution—an academic and administrative adaptiveness goal.
2. To improve the quality of research—an academic adaptiveness goal.
3. To improve the general quality of instruction through the use of the computer in all areas—an academic adaptiveness and production volume goal.
4. To improve the quality of administrative staff work and administrative decision making—an administrative adaptiveness and production volume goal.
5. To provide instructional services in computer science and data processing courses—an academic production volume goal.
6. To reduce administrative expense—an administrative production efficiency goal.

From this ranking one can derive the actual goals as they are perceived by the administrative staff. This process is important since the center's stated goals may be different from its actual goals (Gross, 1969).

The second section of this questionnaire deals with the staff's perception of the effectiveness of the computing center. Here, seven aspects of effectiveness are rated. The first three are general indicators, while the last four are Hage's variables. The language for the last four questions is similar to the computing center indicators presented in Table 1. The general nature of the rated items is as follows:

- Overall effectiveness
- Overall academic service
- Overall administrative service
- Adaptiveness
- Level of production volume
- Production efficiency
- Ability to maintain employee job satisfaction

In evaluating effectiveness on these items, a Lickert-type scale was employed. The scale had five points labeled Excellent, Very Good, Good, Fair, and Poor.

3. The Faculty-Perceived Operational Goal Instrument. This questionnaire measures the faculty's perception of the computing center's goals in terms of Hage's variables as well as their perception of the computing center's effectiveness in meeting these goals. The questionnaire is identical in approach to the staff-perceived operational goal instrument.

4. The Student-Perceived Operational Goal Instrument. This questionnaire measures the student's perception of the computing center's effectiveness in terms of Hage's variables. Students were not asked to rank the goals of the center since they were not familiar with these issues. In addition, they were not asked to rate the center's ability to maintain employee job satisfaction. As a result, this instrument is identical in approach to the staff-perceived operational goal instrument except for the elimination of the first section of rankings and the last item in the second section of ratings.

Data Collection

The data collection procedures for this study are summarized below. These procedures are general and can be used to replicate this study or to conduct similar effectiveness measurement studies (Varanelli and Sugarman, 1979). Ten university computing centers were assessed.

1. A structured interview, conducted by an expert observer, is held with the chief administrator of the computing center.

2. During the structured interview, the measure-of-performance instrument is completed. As indicated before, this questionnaire involves the collection of operational data such as input and output volumes, budget information, staffing and equipment configurations, and so on.

3. During the structured interview, a list of the major users of the computing service is compiled. Specific criteria, such as level of use, service requirements, and priority users, are employed to identify major users.

4. Major administrative and academic users are asked to fill out their respective perceived operational goal instruments.

5. A sample of students is asked to complete the student-perceived operational goal instrument.

Development of Effectiveness Measures

In evaluating the effectiveness of an institution, one must generally combine the assessment items in some fashion. In this study, items from the four data-gathering instruments were combined so that four major components of effectiveness emerged. These four effectiveness measures are listed below:

1. *Academic Operational Effectiveness.* This measure deals with the academic effectiveness of the computing center as indicated by operational data derived from the measure-of-performance instrument.

2. *Perceived Academic Effectiveness.* This measure deals with the perception of all computer users at the university regarding the computing center's academic effectiveness. A weighted combination of the perceptions of administrators, faculty, and students, as obtained from their respective perceived operational goal instruments, comprises this measure.

3. *Administrative Operational Effectiveness.* This measure deals with the administrative effectiveness of the computing center as indicated by operational data derived from the measure-of-performance instrument.

4. *Perceived Administrative Effectiveness.* This measure deals with the perception of all computer users at the university regarding the computing center's administrative effectiveness. A weighted combination of the perceptions of administrators, faculty, and students, as obtained from their respective perceived operational goal instruments, comprises this measure.

Each of the above measures represents an overall assessment of the computing center's effectiveness in terms of Hage's variables and the center's derived goals. Basically, the difference between the average ranking of specific goals by users and their average ratings of the center's effectiveness on the same goals comprises part of the two perceptual measures. User ratings of overall effectiveness are also considered. In addition, the rankings and ratings on the perceptual instruments are weighted according to the relative number of academic and administrative users. For example, if more users are administrative than academic, then their perceptions of the university computing center are given more weight.

Likewise, the operational measures are also weighted and combined. These measures are averages that are weighted by two values called the academic weight and the administrative weight. These weights express the distribution of hardware and personnel costs for academic and administrative computing on a per student basis.

In addition, it was necessary to normalize items comprising these measures so that comparable operational and perceptual measures could be obtained between institutions. The normalization of perceptual measures involved a weighting that reflected the number of full-time equivalent faculty and full-time equivalent students residing at each institution. The normalization of operational measures involved a normalization of all hardware costs, regardless of financial arrangement at the individual institution, to the extended lease plan (ELP) financial terms offered by the vendors of the hardware configuration in question. ELP data were obtained from either the DATAPRO reference manuals or from appropriate vendors.

As can be seen, then, investigators interested in assessing the effectiveness of an institution must derive some method for optimally combining and weighting the data. This method should ensure that the institution's ability to meet the derived goals is fairly appraised. The method used in this study is similar to that used by Georgopoulos and Mann (1962) and involves the development of complex mathematical models. In addition, when institutions are compared, it is important that their effectiveness measures be as comparable as possible. Budgeted funds and number of users of a service may reflect critical differences between institutions. These differences require that measures be normalized in order to remove biases.

Analysis of Data

The evaluation of the effectiveness of computing centers at the ten institutions participating in this study required that the four measures of effectiveness for each institution be converted to ranks. Table 2 lists the ranks each of the universities received on the four derived measures of effectiveness discussed in the previous section. In addition to listing the relative effectiveness rankings of the institutions, the table also shows the sum of the ranks and the average ranks of the participating institutions.

An examination of the table below shows that University J, which was ranked seventh in perceived administrative effectiveness, first in perceived academic effectiveness, second in administrative operational effectiveness, and first in academic operational effectiveness, had a rank sum of 11 and an average rank of 2.75, for an overall effectiveness ranking of one. The highest rank sum was that developed for University C. This institution had a rank sum of 35 and an average rank of 8.75. This was the least effective university computing center. Its average rank is over 300 percent greater than that achieved by University J.

To get a first-order indication of the reliability of the effectiveness measures, one may evaluate the differences between the sum of the operational measures and the sum of the perceptual measures. For example, for

Table 2. Effectiveness Rankings for All Institutions

Effectiveness Measures	University									
	A	B	C	D	E	F	G	H	I	J
Perceived Administrative	8	10	9	3	6	2	1	5	4	7
Perceived Academic	6	8	10	7	9	2	3	5	4	1
Administrative Operations	1	8	7	3	4	6	10	5	9	2
Academic Operations	2	3	9	5	7	8	10	4	6	1
Sum of Ranks	17	29	35	18	26	18	24	19	23	11
Average of Ranks	4.25	7.25	8.75	4.50	6.50	4.50	6.00	4.75	5.75	2.75

University J, the sum of the operational measures is 3, and the sum of the perceptual measures is 8. Therefore the absolute value of the difference between these measures is 5. If the rank difference for all institutions is computed, two distinct groups emerge. One group has relatively low differences in perceptual and operational measures and one group has large differences in these measures. The first group is formed by Universities B, C, D, E, H, I and J. For these seven institutions, the average difference between the perceptual measures and the operational measures is 4.14. For Universities A, F and G, the average difference is 12.33. These figures suggest that in the first group of universities, there is a fairly good congruence between the operational and perceptual effectiveness measures. For the second grouping this congruence is quite limited.

A rank correlation was computed between the rankings of the individual measures of effectiveness and the overall effectiveness ranking for the first group, Universities B, C, D, E, H, I and J. The results are shown in Table 3. The perceived academic measure is significantly correlated with the final rankings if alpha is assigned its traditional value of .05. However, all measures tended to be associated with the final rankings for the seven universities considered. Of course, because there are so few universities in the sample, it is difficult to reach the traditionally accepted criterion of significance of .05, even though the correlations reported are moderate if one takes into account the differing nature of the measures. In addition, it is not necessary from a theoretical standpoint that these four measures be substantially homogeneous. Although there is some indication that they may be homogeneous measures of computing center effectiveness, greater heterogeneity might simply indicate that computing center effectiveness should be considered from all four vantage points and not as a whole. In fact, the operating environment of the three universities not considered here (A, F, and G) was so atypical that it precluded any significant association between perceptual and operational measures and made necessary the independent consideration of each measure. Indeed, major differences between perceptual and operational measures can be significant of themselves.

Table 3. Rank Correlation Coefficients for Individual Effectiveness Measures with Final Ranking for Selected Institutions

Effectiveness Measures	di^2	Correlation Measures rs	Pr^a
Perceived Administrative	46.25	+.175	36%
Perceived Academic	18.25	+.675	5%
Administrative Operations	39.25	+.32	26%
Academic Operations	41.25	+.28	30%

[a]Pr = Probability that ranks are independent

Conclusions

This study demonstrates the use of the derived goal approach to measure the effectiveness of computing centers where a single computing center serves all components of an organization. Moreover, the derived goal approach may provide a means for assessing the effectiveness of many organizational stituations where competing user groups are vying for the use of scarce resources and where department goals are clear and measurable. This study overcomes one of the major criticisms of the goal approach by providing for an empirical method for the identification and measurement of organizational goals (Price, 1972).

The final effectiveness rankings for the ten computing centers studied in this project are considered by the author a true indication of the relative merit of operations at each of the centers. The rankings also show that the power of the model lies in its ability to highlight areas of computer center performance that must be changed in order to improve the overall effectiveness of the center. The model can pinpoint difficulties in user group interactions, goal perception, hardware limitations, organizational structure, and so on. If used as a tool by managers, the research model may serve as a blueprint for improving effectiveness in computing centers.

The power of the model is clearly demonstrated by the case of University A. This school showed a wide variance between the user's perception of the center's effectiveness and the effectiveness as judged by the center's operational characteristics. The users perceived the center as being relatively ineffective, whereas, operationally, the contrary appeared to be true. Further analysis of the data indicates that there is little agreement between user groups and the computing center management about the overall goals of the center. Perhaps the perception of effectiveness could be improved if university management undertook a program to evaluate the goals of the center and, to the extent possible, make these goals coincide with the desires of various user groups.

24

References

Etzioni, A. *A Comparative Analysis of Complex Organizations.* New York: Free Press, 1975.

Fedrick, R. J. "A Study of the Organization and Administration of Computer Services in California Public Junior Colleges and Their Relationship to Effectiveness." Unpublished doctoral dissertation, Department of Educational Administration, University of California, Los Angeles, 1971.

Fleckenstein, D. "Role Conflict of University Computing Center Directors as Related to Computing Center Effectiveness." Unpublished doctoral dissertation, Department of Educational Administration, University of Wisconsin, 1972.

Georgopoulos, B. S., and Mann, F. C. *The Community General Hospital.* New York: MacMillan, 1962.

Gross, E. "The Definition of Organizational Goals." *British Journal of Sociology,* 1969, *20*, 277–294.

Hage, J. "An Axiomatic Theory of Organizations." *Administrative Science Quarterly,* 1965, *10*, 289–320.

Ivey, W. Unpublished and uncopyrighted questionnaire. Arizona State University, 1972.

Nunnally, J. C. *Psychometric Theory.* New York: McGraw-Hill, 1967.

Price, J. L. "The Study of Organizational Effectiveness." *The Scoiological Quarterly,* 1972, *13*, 3–15.

Steers, R. M. *Organizational Effectiveness: A Behavioral View.* Santa Monica, Calif.: Goodyear, 1977.

Varanelli, A., and Sugarman, M. *Evaluation Study of Performance of Stamford Area CETA Administration Training and Employment Programs.* Stamford: State of Connecticut Department of Labor, 1979.

Andrew Varanelli, Jr. is professor and chairman,
Undergraduate Department of Management,Lubin Schools of
Business Administration, Pace University, New York City. He
has been a consultant, teacher, and practitioner in the field of
data processing and information science for seventeen years
and has served as director of the Pace University computing
center.

*New York State's attempt to base salaries on
performance illustrates the many problems that
attend this type of employee appraisal system.*

Assessing Performance-Based Salary Administration in the Public Sector

Patrick J. Bulgaro
Meyer S. Frucher

In any meeting room where public personnel administrators gather, performance evaluation, as a purely philosophical idea, can generate a lively discussion. But once implemented in the workplace, performance evaluation can illustrate the classic gap between theory and practice. Public administrators in New York State have learned that lesson. The state's experience with performance evaluation during 1980 has been at once exhilarating and agonizing.

When the concept of performance-based salary administration was first seriously broached, as the state was about to enter negotiations on 1979 contracts with employee unions, it seemed to offer a panacea for an array of knotty and long-standing problems. The existing compensation system was a hybrid. It combined negotiated, across-the-board pay raises with a relic called increments. Increments were nothing more than an administrative device to move an employee from the hiring rate to the average job rate over a five-year period.

D. Baugher (Ed.). *New Directions for Program Evaluation: Measuring Effectiveness*, no. 11.
San Francisco: Jossey-Bass, September 1981

Increments were worth $22.5 million a year to the employees who got them. Yet increments did not buy the state improved work performance. In fact, increments may have cost the state some of its better workers. Such flat-rate systems have been shown to cause dissatisfaction in high performers and at the same time foster satisfaction in low performers (Baird and Hamner, 1979; Fossum, 1979).

Given the demotivating nature of the state's system of compensation, many administrators in New York believed that a performance evaluation system that could transform the increments into a merit raise, combined with an award system, would be quite useful. First, such a system might help motivate the majority of employers already at the job rate. Second, it could help the state overcome its recruitment and retention difficulties, caused by the state's lagging salaries in comparison to the private sector, by promising high performers fast acceleration through the salary schedule. Third, a flexible compensation system could ease the high turnover and low morale problems common in prisons and mental institutions, where the state often assumes the role of employer of last resort. Finally, the system could give supervisors a needed tool to reward, to withhold rewards, to force face-to-face discussions between themselves and subordinates about mutual job and performance expectations, and to serve to identify training needs. In short, the new performance-based compensation system offered a promise to breathe new life into the personnel system.

Labor Relations and Compensation: The Climate in New York

Salaries and benefits for New York state employees, which during the 1960s and early 1970s were competitive with private sector and other governmental organizations, began to drop significantly in the mid 1970s. This transition from feast to famine for the state and its employees couldn't have been more dramatic than in 1975 and 1976. With the threatened bankruptcy of New York City and collapse of the state Urban Development Corporation, the state's economic viability was thrown into question.

Employees in bargaining units with expiring contracts went without pay raises for those two years, save for a one-shot $250 bonus one year. Job security went out the window as thousands of state employees were laid off. The state bought further trouble for itself in 1977 during negotiations on new two-year contracts. When negotiations were concluded, New York in effect had two salary schedules for most bargaining units. One schedule guaranteed raises of 9 percent over the life of the 1977–79 contract for employees already on the payroll. The other reimbursed employees hired during the new contract period at 1976–77 levels. Although this arrangement produced immediate financial savings for the state, it hampered the state's recruiting efforts by treating new hires as second-class employees.

Given this history, the unions arrived at the bargaining table in 1979 demanding double digit percent pay raises to match inflation and to recoup losses from the lean years of 1975–76. Additionally, the salary schedule, which for most bargaining units was based on five increment steps in each grade from the hiring rate to the job rate, presented another disturbing problem to the unions. Generally, more than half of the workers were earning the maximum or above the maximum for their salary grade. As a result, the majority of employees who earned the maximum for their salary grade were shut out from any consideration simply because of where they fit in the salary schedule. Employees earning below the job rate were eligible for both negotiated and incremental raises based strictly on time-in-salary grade, whether their performance was mediocre or superior. In order to circumvent the lock-step system, employees earning the maximum for their salary grade often attempted to have their jobs reclassified to a higher grade through the Department of Civil Service's Division of Classification and Compensation.

From management's view, the existing compensation system was disturbing as well. It was devoid of any tools to motivate employees to improve performance or boost productivity. The compensation system simply acted as a sieve to funnel money to employees. So, in 1979, the state went to the bargaining table with the express purpose of building productivity incentives into the compensation plan.

As a result, both management and the unions were ready for some change in the compensation system when bargaining began in 1979, although their predispositions for change did not have the same basis. The unions were interested in maximum increases for as many workers as possible, whereas management wanted a method to reward better performers. Fortunately, management found an unexpected ally in the President's Council on Wage and Price Stability (COWPS). COWPS would not exclude increment payments from the voluntary 7 percent wage increase guidelines. In other words, if the fixed increments stayed, COWPS would view payments as compensation to be charged against pay raises. However, COWPS indicated that merit payments would be permitted outside of the guidelines.

With this verdict, the three unions that did not already have merit-based compensation plans — The Civil Employees Association (CSEA), Public Employees Federation, and Council 82 — accepted the concept of performance evaluation to replace increments. The concept was also built into the compensation plan for management/confidential employees.

The Workforce

As shown in Table 1, the state's workforce of 190,000 employees under the control of the Executive Branch is as diverse as it is large. There are some 6,900 different job titles in the classified state service. The mode

28

Table 1. New York State's Work Force

Management/Confidential (M/C)	Covers 7,500 managers and 3,000 confidential employees. Designation includes those who formulate policy, help prepare for or conduct contract negotiations, play major roles in administering contracts or major roles in personnel administration or assist managers with those responsibilities in a confidential capacity.
Civil Service Employees Association American Federation of State, County and Municipal Employees, (AFSCME), AFL-CIO	Largest state worker union, representing 105,000 employees in three units: Administrative Services, including clerks, typists and stenographers; Institutional Services, composed of therapy aides and others in direct care roles in mental hygiene facilities, youth camps and drug treatment centers; Operational Services, representing maintenance helpers, plumbers, and construction equipment operators.
Council 82, American Federation of State, County and Municipal Employees (AFSCME), AFL-CIO	Represents two units: The 10,000-worker Security Services Unit of correction, conservation and security officers plus capitol police, and the 200-member Security Supervisors Unit covering prison system lieutenants and captains.
Public Employees Federation, AFL-CIO	Represents the 45,000-member Professional, Scientific and Technical Services unit which includes head clerks and stenographers in grades 23 and below, and various job categories in grade 24 and above, such as accountants, auditors, counselors, civil engineers, lawyers, nurses, psychologists, and physicians.
Police Benevolent Association of the New York State Police Troopers, Inc.	Represents 2,500 troopers, 600 investigators and 570 commissioned and noncommissioned officers, split in three separate bargaining units.
United University Professions, Inc., New York State United Teachers, American Federation of Teachers, AFL-CIO	Represents the 16,500-member faculty and non-teaching professional staff in the State University of New York system.

among job titles is mental hygiene therapy aide. Twenty thousand employees working at the state's psychiatric and mental retardation facilities hold this job. Nearly half, or 3,400, of the job titles are applied to only one individual. Among the more exotic one-of-a-kind titles are kosher food inspector and supervisor of mineral water baths at Saratoga Spa.

Skills needed for the jobs vary greatly; there are highly trained cancer research scientists and sweepers. Salaries range from $6,810 a year for domestic and locker room attendants to a possible $104,000 (in combined state pay and earnings from approved clinical practice plans) for certain medical school faculty.

Less than 6 percent of the executive branch employees are designated managerial/confidential and are thus barred from union membership and representation. Traditionally, management/confidential employees have been treated as tag-alongs, receiving carbon-copy wage increases and benefit improvements of those negotiated by unions for the employees they represent. The rest, 94.3 percent, are unionized, including some 25,000 first- and second-line supervisors who in the private sector would be considered a part of the management team.

The unionized employees are divided into ten bargaining units, which follow broad job categories. The ten units in turn are represented at the negotiating table and in contract and disciplinary actions and grievances by the five employee unions.

The Experiment

Four employee groups were involved in the implementation of the performance-based compensation system. These were the management/confidential, CSEA, Council 82, and the Public Employees Federation groups.

Management/Confidential. The performance evaluation system for management/confidential personnel was designed to give management broad discretion and flexibility in setting salary levels to recognize differences in employee performance. The system used five rating categories and was applied both to employees earning below and above the job rate for their salary grades. Advancement-eligible employees rated "superior" could receive anywhere from 26 to 40 percent of the dollar difference between the hiring rate and the job rate every six months. Those rated as performing "above expected level" were eligible for between 18 to 25 percent of the dollar range. A rating of "at expected level" permitted payment of between 5 and 17 percent of the range. Employees rated "below expected level" and "below minimum level" were ineligible for advancements. Cash awards ranging from $500 to a maximum of 5 percent of salary were available to employees earning at or above the job rate. An amount equaling 1 percent of the total management/confidential payroll was appropriated to finance the awards.

CSEA. The plan for employees in the three CSEA-represented bargaining units was devised by a joint labor-management task force. The plan was based on a four-step rating system — outstanding, highly effective, satisfactory, and needs substantial improvement. Depending upon their ratings, advancement-eligible employees could move through the salary schedule at fast, regular, or slow paces. Because the schedule for each salary grade had been compressed from five to four steps, it was now possible for an employee to move from the hiring rate to the job rate in eighteen months if he or she consistently received the two highest ratings based on six-month evaluations. Employees rated "satisfactory" would advance through the schedule at one-year intervals; those rated "needs substantial improvement" would be ineligible for advancement for one year.

Performance awards of $300 were available to employees earning at or above the job rate for their salary grade. Some $4.8 million, or 1 percent of the CSEA payroll, was made available to cover 25 percent of the award-eligible employees. The money was distributed proportionately by bargaining unit, agency, and work location.

Council 82. A joint committee of management and union representatives devised a performance evaluation plan for uniformed security personnel, who rejected the concepts of bonuses and acceleration to accommodate union wishes. A bonus system would have meant an end to the ten- and fifteen-year longevity payments, which in the union's view were untouchable. Faster acceleration through the advancement steps also was tossed aside because union members feared that supervisors would base their judgments on favoritism rather than merit.

Instead, the union accepted a semi-yearly evaluation of employees. Ten different work factors were evaluated, ranging from guards' response in emergency situations, punctuality and attendance, report preparation, and knowledge of rules and regulations to relationships with fellow employees and clientele groups. With this system, supervisors assign a numerical rating from 1 to 3 to describe the employee's performance level for each of ten work factors. The numbers are then totaled to arrive at one of five adjective ratings. To receive the highest rating, "outstanding," an employee must receive 27–30 points; employees accumulating 23–26 points receive a rating of "excellent"; 18–22 points draw a rating of "good"; 15–17 points indicate "needs improvement"; and 10–14 points translate into a rating of "unsatisfactory." All employees in the bargaining unit are rated, no matter whether they are advancement-eligible or not, although only those earning below the job rate who receive the four highest ratings get the performance advancements. The size depends upon the salary grade.

Public Employees Federation. The performance evaluation system for this group of employees was developed in late September 1980 by a joint labor-management committee. The union rejected an award component in favor of "enrichment" of the job rates by $300 to $500 in two steps during the life of the three-year contract. The new system will treat employees in one of two ways based on their grade level and will differentiate performance levels in three categories.

Employees in grades 23 and below are eligible for performance advances equaling one third of the range for their salary grade. Those rated in the lowest performance category are ineligible for advances. Those rated in the middle category will receive one advance for the year equal to one third of the salary range. Employees rated in the top category are eligible for two advances during the year, each pegged at one third of the range.

Employees in grade 24 and above will be paid on a "variable" rate basis, which gives managers and supervisors more flexibility to recognize an individual's performance. Under this plan, managers will assign each employee to one of three broad performance categories and then recommend a specific percentage advance within the range for that category. Employees rated in the top two categories will be eligible to receive advances during the year totaling anywhere from 25 to 80 percent of the range. Employees in the lowest category will not be eligible for advances.

The two sides agreed to a narrative performance program for each employee. The supervisor, after consulting with the employee, will describe performance objectives, standards, and goals. The performance programs will be used as the basis for supervisory assessment of the employee's performance for the six-month period.

Appeals. Appeals mechanisms were built into all of the systems to give employees dissatisfied with their ratings a chance to question their supervisors' assessments of their performance and make a case for raising the evaluations. The process for all systems generally follows a three-step review. Final review is by a three-member statewide appeal board consisting of a union representative, a representative from management, and a neutral party.

The Implementation Effort

The time schedule for developing specifics on the performance evaluation programs was thrown off by a sixteen-day strike by Council 82 and its aftermath. Because of the American Federation of State, County, and Municipal Employees (AFSCME) family tie, the leadership of CSEA held up counting members' votes awaiting ratification of the union's contract throughout the Council 82 strike. That delay, in turn, contributed to delays in submitting legislation authorizing the new compensation plans for CSEA, Council 82, and management/confidential employees to the state legislature until the final days of the legislative session in June 1979.

Throughout the summer, work proceeded on development of the management/confidential and CSEA plans. The idea was that training for both programs would be conducted simultaneously. But, because of snags in negotiations on the CSEA plan, which were not finalized until the end of September, the training did not begin until mid-October.

The evaluations of employees by their immediate supervisors were conducted in November 1979, a schedule that left little time to adequately train all levels of supervisors who would be involved in the program. The training period opened with a letter by Governor Hugh L. Carey to all department and agency heads. The letter stressed the administration's hopes for the program and asked for the leadership's full attention to make the program work.

The training was a "filtering down" operation. The core group of trainers was a task force of thirty-six negotiators and professional staff members from the Governor's Office of Employee Relations and key agency employee relations officers who underwent thorough indoctrination in the program. The task force in turn divided into smaller teams to conduct "train-the-trainer" sessions in seven areas across the state. Five thousand personnel administrators and top supervisors selected by agencies and departments participated in the sessions. These trainers then returned to their respective agencies, institutions, and workplaces to train immediate supervisors in the workings of the system.

Managers and supervisors at all levels were given manuals and evaluation sheets explaining the program and outlining the evaluation procedures completely. With that, the evaluations were under way. Supervisors typically evaluated from one to twenty employees.

Early Results

Indications that all was not well with the first round of evaluations were soon apparent. The Governor's Office of Employee Relations—the agency responsible for negotiating and overseeing implementation of contracts—and the Division of the Budget, which shared monitoring responsibilities, began receiving reports early in December from individual operating agencies. It was apparent that the ratings were extremely favorable to the employees being rated.

CSEA Results. Based on the experience of performance evaluation systems in use in the private sector, the two agencies had expected 10 percent of the CSEA employees to be rated "outstanding," 15 percent to be rated "highly effective" and the majority, or 65 percent, to be rated "satisfactory." Ten percent were expected to receive rating of "needs substantial improvement." The ratings for CSEA produced 13 percent at the "outstanding" level, 35 percent at "highly effective," only 48 percent of "satisfactory," and 1 percent at "needing substantial improvement."

Efforts to control the runaway ratings were met by accusations by CSEA members that the state was setting "quotas," and these charges soon found their way into the public print. With that, the dissension spread, and a moratorium on the CSEA plan was called in early January 1980, with plans to revise the system.

Management/Confidential Results. Early reports on the distribution of ratings for the management/confidential group were even more disappointing than early reports on the CSEA ratings. One department rated 90 percent of its advancement-eligible employees and 100 percent of its award-eligible employees in the top two categories. Still, the management/confidential evaluations were continuing. Governor Carey again wrote agency heads and commissioners to warn them that a unique opportunity to experiment with a flexible, performance-based compensation system would slip from management's hands unless they devoted their personal attention to making it work. When the warnings and supplementary guidelines failed to stem the tide of high ratings, the Division of the Budget and Office of Employee Relations instituted a contingency plan in a budget bulletin issued February 6, 1980. The plan required all agencies to submit a summary of their ratings and proposed payments for review by the two central agencies.

Agencies whose proposed ratings significantly exceeded the guidelines were asked to justify the ratings. Agencies that failed to adequately substantiate the results were told that the ratings would be rejected and returned for further clarification and revision. In any event, no money would be paid out until the entire agency submission was approved.

Of sixty agencies and departments, only 48 percent (that is, twenty-nine agencies) submitted plans that were approved without change. The other agencies were given two options for final clearance. The first choice was to numerically rank management/confidential employees receiving the two highest ratings. The Division of Budget and Office of Employee Relations then reviewed the lists, and using statewide guidelines, set cutoff points. Under this option, the top 37.5 percent of the advancement-eligible employees received maximum reimbursement, while the rest were treated as if they had received ratings of "at expected level." Awards were limited to the top 16 percent. The second option, selected by most agencies, covered more employees but meant fewer dollars in their pockets. Under this option, everyone whose rating qualified them for an advancement received the minimum amount available for their salary range, and 24 percent of the qualified award-eligible employees were paid $500 per person. During July 1980, the management/confidential compensation program was put on hold for revision.

Council 82 Results. By contrast, the performance evaluation system for Council 82 employees proceeded with no major problems. Supervisors had received extensive training by the time the evaluations were conducted in May and June of 1980. In addition, union officials gave the program enthusiastic support. They viewed the face-to-face meetings between supervisor and employee as a plus to further supervisor understanding of the problems of officers. Nonetheless, at this writing, the results of Council 82 ratings have not been thoroughly evaluated.

Public Employees Federation Results. The performance evaluation system for this group was developed in late September 1980. The first evaluations for Public Employees Federation-represented employees will begin in April 1981. As such, the results of this system are not available at this time.

Conclusions

As can be seen, many problems emerged in the implementation of the new performance based compensation systems. To be sure, the crash training program was a major part of the problem. If a more thorough training program could have been implemented initially, the errors of leniency found may have been reduced (Ivancevich, 1979). Of course, no one expected that the state's first experience with performance evaluation would proceed without hitches. The transition from a lock-step increment system to a performance-based compensation system was a major undertaking. Supervisors were not used to, or prepared for, such authority. Employees, no matter where they fit in the hierarchy in state government, were accustomed to thinking of salary increments as a right rather than something to work for through achievement. It was overly optimistic to rely on admittedly untrained supervisors to make appropriate use of the evaluation tool that was handed to them.

The CSEA program also contained a basic mechanical flaw. The "satisfactory" rating, which ranked third from the top on a scale of four adjectives, apparently carried a negative connotation in the minds of some supervisors and employees. The other possibility is that the adjective itself was a poor choice, failing to accurately describe the employee who consistently and competently performs his or her assigned duties.

As a result, some changes in the CSEA system were made in the summer of 1980. The new system differs in three major respects. First, employees will now be rated with one of three adjectives—outstanding, effective, or unsatisfactory. Second, immediate supervisors will continue to be responsible for appraising the performance of their subordinates, but they no longer will assign the ratings. Instead, after the appraisal, the supervisor will meet with the next-level supervisor, who will assign a tentative rating. The evaluations will then be submitted to first-level management for review and assignment of a final rating. Third, when this evaluation process is completed, the immediate supervisor will meet with the employee to explain the basis for the rating and discuss the employee's strengths and areas needing improvement. The expectation is that this process will remove pressure from the immediate supervisor and ensure uniformity in application and equitable treatment of employees. In order to aid the process, a comprehensive training program has been completed that involved all management and supervisory levels. Supervisors received in-depth training in task identification and face-to-face discussion techniques with employees.

It is difficult to determine exactly why the management/confidential ratings suffered problems of leniency as well. While the adjectives in this system were more precise in defining performance levels, a rating of "at expected level" could be equated in the minds of supervisors as a collegiate C on a scale of A–F and therefore regarded as mediocre or undistinguished. A five-adjective system might be too ambitious, requiring supervisors to make fine-tuned distinctions that are not defensible without more sensitive measurement standards and instruments.

The efforts to control runaway ratings in the management/confidential system gave rise to a still unresolved argument among those involved in reshaping the system. The argument turns on a sensitive question: Should money drive the system? In theory, the evaluations should reflect an employee's performance without regard to financial considerations. If all employees are outstanding, they should be rewarded appropriately. However, the argument can be made that dollars must be used as a restraint. Otherwise, there is little incentive for agencies to rate realistically and avoid excessive cost. For their part, a number of agencies have indicated that they want to know beforehand how much money is available so as to avoid painful choices later.

Those who argue for cash incentives say that money should augment praise. Money has a practical value; dollars mean more than nice words. These individuals are certainly correct to a certain extent. Monetary incentives do seem to lead to greater employee commitment and increased performance (Latham, Mitchell, and Dossett, 1978; Terborg and Miller, 1978; Tolchinsky and King, 1980; Wofford, 1979). Nonetheless, other factors are equal to money, if not more important than money, in sustaining increased performance in workers. In fact, the impact of monetary incentives on work output seems much less than that of setting difficult concrete goals (Latham, Mitchell, and Dossett, 1978). There are many theories of motivation that suggest that money may not be the prime motivator (Campbell, 1976). In the case of workers in prisons (for example, Council 82 workers), it may be that money is much less motivating for them than for other workers in the state. These workers seem more interested in improving their stressful work environment than getting pay increases (Muchinsky and Maassarani, 1980).

But the fact is that many of these other motivational forces—such as meaningful work—are not neatly handled within the framework of a labor-management contract. Merit pay for good performance is. Of course, the details of such a system require time and patience to work out. Performance evaluation requires the commitment and daily involvement of the entire chain-of-command from the governor on down (Ivancevich, 1972; Ivancevich, 1974; Ivancevich and others, 1970). New York's first try might have turned out differently if commissioners and agency heads had been held personally accountable and been made to see a tie-in between performance evaluation and achievement of agency goals. It would have been useful to have supervisors themselves evaluated, in part, on the quality of their ratings.

The ultimate lesson from the New York state experience is that there is a pressing need for research and experimentation to improve performance evaluation measurement techniques. The state of the art in personnel assessment is presently primitive, at best. Yet it is questionable just how exact such a system can ever be in the public sector. For better or worse, public administrators seem doomed to function in an environment that lacks the precision and discipline of the "balance sheet" of private industry. Social programs aimed at broad and noble purposes will continue to exist and elude efforts to devise definitive measures of effectiveness. In some areas, political objectives or swift societal change will blur program purposes. Moreover, a portion of the bureaucracy, at least, will remain impervious to redirection and unresponsive to needs perceived by management.

In this atmosphere, the success of a performance assessment system will necessarily depend on whether a complementary system of defining management objectives can be devised and enforced and on whether broad policy objectives can be translated into specific tasks and duties for the smallest organizational unit, and ultimately, for the individual employee. Through the interactions of these systems a dialogue could be created whereby management would articulate its needs and employees would gain a knowledge of their role in the organization. Salary compensation programs geared to measurement of how well or poorly that role is carried out could well hold the promise of substantially altering the dynamics of employment within the public sector. New York state has taken a modest step in that direction.

References

Baird, L. S., and Hamner, W. "Individual Versus Systems Rewards: Who's Dissatisfied, Why, and What Is Their Likely Response?" *Academy of Management Journal*, 1979, *22*, 783–792.

Campbell, J. P. "Motivation Theory in Industrial and Organizational Psychology." In M. Dunnette (Ed.), *Handbook of Industrial and Organizational Psychology*. Chicago: Rand McNally, 1976.

Fossum, J. A. "The Effects of Positively and Negatively Contingent Rewards and Individual Differences on Performance, Satisfaction, and Expectations." *Academy of Management Journal*, 1979, *22*, 577–589.

Ivancevich, J. M. "A Longitudinal Assessment of Management by Objectives." *Administrative Science Quarterly*, 1972, *17*, 126–138.

Ivancevich, J. M. "Changes in Performance in a Management by Objectives Program." *Administrative Science Quarterly*, 1974, *19*, 563–574.

Ivancevich, J. M. "Longitudinal Study of the Effects of Rater Training on Psychometric Error in Ratings." *Journal of Applied Psychology*, 1979, *64*, 502–508.

Ivancevich, J. M., Donnelly, J. H., and Lyon, H. H. "A Study of the Impact of Management by Objectives on Perceived Need Satisfaction." *Personnel Psychology*, 1970, *23*, 139–151.

Latham, G. P., Mitchell, T. R., and Dossett, L. "Importance of Participative Goal Setting and Anticipated Rewards on Goal Difficulty and Job Performance." *Journal of Applied Psychology*, 1978, *63*, 163–171.

Muchinsky, P. M., and Maassarani, M. A. "Work Environment Effects on Public Sector Grievances. *Personnel Psychology*, 1980, *33*, 403–414.

Terborg, J. R., and Miller, H. E. "Motivation, Behavior, and Performance: A Closer Examination of Goal Setting and Monetary Incentives." *Journal of Applied Psychology,* 1978, *63,* 29–39.

Tolchinsky, P. D., and King, D. C. "Do Goals Mediate the Effects of Incentives on Performance?" *Academy of Management Review,* 1980, *5,* 455–467.

Wofford, J. C. "A Goal-Energy-Effort Requirement Model of Work Motivation." *Academy of Management Review,* 1979, *4,* 193–201.

Patrick J. Bulgaro serves as deputy chief budget examiner for the New York State Division of the Budget. He has fiscal responsibility for negotiation and administration of collective bargaining agreements for executive branch employees. Mr. Bulgaro was formerly on the faculty of Siena College.

As director of the New York State Office of Employee Relations, Meyer S. Frucher serves as the governor's agent in negotiating and administering collective bargaining agreements covering nearly 175,000 executive branch employees in New York state. From 1975 until 1978, he was executive director of the New York State Commission on Management and Productivity in the Public Sector.

The clinical programs that test psychotropic drugs
are strictly monitored in accordance with procedural
and research guidelines.

Evaluating Clinical
Investigation of
Psychotropic Substances

J. R. Wittenborn
Frances O. Kelsey

The effectiveness of a research organization, like the effectiveness of a manufacturing organization, may be gauged by the quality of the product and the acceptance of the product on the market. The present chapter considers the effectiveness of programs of clinical research aimed at determining the merit of substances of psychopharmacotherapeutic potential. The product generated by this research is information, and its utility is in large measure a function of the manner in which it is generated.

There are many ways in which a substance of potential psychotropic utility may evolve, but there is only one path by which such a substance may come to lawful therapeutic application in the United States. This is by claims of efficacy and safety based on clinical investigation acceptable to the Food and Drug Administration (FDA).

The market for information concerning substances designed for psychopharmacotherapeutic purposes, not unlike the market for other products, proceeds in a series of important steps. The first step in the market sequence of information concerning drug effects is acceptance by the FDA. The second step is acceptance of this information by the

D. Baugher (Ed.). *New Directions for Program Evaluation: Measuring Effectiveness*, no. 11.
San Francisco: Jossey-Bass, September 1981

prescribing physicians, and the third step is acceptance by the patient. In the final analysis, the resulting product is an integration, if not a compromise of the demands of the market and the provisions of the required research procedures for documenting safety and efficacy.

It is no exaggeration to state that the procedures used to document the quality and safety of the psychotropic substance define its fundamental essence. It is not surprising, therefore, to discover that the market demands procedural documentation. The producing organization, whether an investigational team working in isolation or a large pharmaceutical company engaged in a standard program of multiple investigations, must assume the burden of maintaining procedural records. More important, these records must meet the serious scrutiny of any qualified person demanding documentation. Any investigation of psychopharmacotherapeutic potential must use procedures known by and acceptable to those who comprise the market, particularly the FDA. Failures to disclose procedures or falsification of procedures will invalidate the informational product, regardless of the actual validity of resulting inferences. It is not permissible to be right for the wrong reasons.

Development of Programmatic Control in Clinical Psychopharmacology

Clinical research has metamorphosed from highly individualized, almost idiosyncratic procedures to a mass-produced commodity. A few decades ago clinical investigators of psychotropic substances selected, if not designed, their own methods, generated their conclusions by means of data summaries with which they were familiar, and interpreted their findings in a manner that might or might not be acceptable to their colleagues. Today, however, much clinical research, certainly the research conducted in the development of new psychotropic drugs, is directed on a programmatic basis and is in effect regulated by criteria developed under the egis of the FDA. This direction and regulatory control of clinical research has meant important methodological advancements in a field where tactics are often managed by personnel trained as clinicians but assigned to research and where research strategies are dictated by some combination of the marketing perceptions of industry leaders and the emergence of new substances from the pharmacology laboratoy.

The Development of Guidelines

To assist the efforts of investigators who strive to generate information in support of claims of therapeutic efficacy and safety, the FDA has supported and sponsored the promulgation of guidelines. These guidelines are a statement of sound practices in clinical research and represent a consensus opinion of clinical investigators. The original United States guidelines were developed by a committee of clinical investigators working under a contract between the FDA and the American College of Neuropsychopharmacology (ACNP). Although these guidelines were developed for the benefit of personnel assigned to the direction and management of a program of research in support of the efficacy and safety of a new drug, the guidelines may have an incidental secondary function. Since they were developed by recognized experts and have the de facto endorsement of the FDA, they provide a common ground when the FDA and a pharmaceutical company are in controversy concerning appropriate research methodology to support claims for the efficacy and safety of new substances. The guidelines are only recommendations by the FDA, however, and are not formal legal requirements. Nevertheless, their existence (U.S. Department of Commerce, 1977; U.S. Department of Health, Education, and Welfare, 1977a; 1977b; 1979a) as public documents does affect the evaluation of psychotropic drug trials.

Since guidelines must recognize the current status of theory, method, and ethical constraints of clinical investigation, they must be subject to review and revision. The FDA has continued to sponsor the reformulation of old guidelines and the evolution of new guidelines for emerging areas of drug development.

After the pioneering effort of the FDA Task Force, a panel of internationally recognized investigators developed "The International Guidelines for the Clinical Investigation of Psychotropic Drugs" (Wittenborn, 1977). With few exceptions, these guidelines are accepted as representative of sound practices in clinical psychopharmacology and to a large extent parallel the originally sponsored FDA guidelines. Any exceptions recognize recent and continuing advances in pharmacodynamics and pharmacokinetics and current uncertainties concerning diagnostic prescriptions and preferred diagnostic conventions. The guidelines are de facto standards for clinical research in psychopharmacology and are recommended by foreign (for example, German and Japanese) regulatory agencies.

Nature of the International Guidelines

The international guidelines are lengthy and specific. In general, they describe the procedural and methodological practices necessary for sound clinical investigation.

Phases of Research. The development of psychotropic drugs follows a series of three research steps. Each phase of research provides the necessary information for the next phase of research; data collected in one phase is relevant to decisions made about the product in the next phase. These three phases of research are described below (Wittenborn, 1977, p. 210–211).

Phase I studies should provide evidence of dose-related pharmacological effects and side-effects in single dose and time-limited multiple dose studies. The subjects may be normal volunteers and/or psychiatric patients. Evidence of drug absorption and excretion is important, and when possible, evidence of distribution and metabolism should be provided. Data documenting drug effects on mood or behavior in normal volunteers or on symptoms in patients are a desirable but not necessary feature of Phase I studies.

Phase II studies are designed to provide reasonable evidence of clinical efficacy and usually proceed from studies not requiring a comparison group to those in which comparison groups are needed to indicate efficacy in defined patient populations. Knowledge of the effective dose and probable side-effects and some indication of therapeutic potential must be obtained from early Phase II studies before formal, controlled studies are worthwhile.

In Phase III, extensive controlled studies are conducted to confirm and extend the implications of Phase II. Phase III seeks evidence of efficacy in a wide range of patient groups and settings and seeks also to identify specific symptoms and patient groups in which the drug is especially effective. Large and numerous samples are usually involved in the work of this phase. In the course of assaying various aspects of efficacy, information about the incidence of both common and rare adverse effects is obtained. Relationships observed in one study between the administration of the investigational drug and any therapeutic effect or adverse somatic or psychiatric events (for example, jaundice, dermatitis, or suicidal attempts) should be confirmed by independent investigators which provide comparisons with alternative medications.

Psychiatric Classification. The lack of clear, quantifiable methods for diagnosing psychiatric illness makes it difficult for investigators to achieve comparable results. As such, the guidelines recommend the use of the World Health Organization classification for each patient. In addition, the intensity and nature of psychopathological features commonly observed in depressed, anxious, and schizophrenic patients should be described for each patient. In the end, these procedures should make explicit the nature of the patients included in the study and the criteria used to exclude patients.

Procedural Documentation. Ultimately, clear documentation of relevant studies is of paramount importance. Without documentation of the sample and the actual course of treatment, a beautiful study can become a wasted effort. In general, then, it is necessary to document (1) the samples studied; (2) the setting in which the treatment occurred; (3) procedures followed during the clinical trial; (4) the case report of each patient; (5) the criterion measures for side effects, laboratory and physical examinations, and psychopathology; and (6) any other influential variables affecting the clinical trial.

Data Analysis. Since statistical analysis of individual patient data provides the foundation for movement through each phase of research to acceptance of the drug, the international guidelines suggest that the data be analyzed and tabulated according to statistical conventions that allow sound interpretation of clinical efficacy. For a single clinical trial or study, this standard is met by (1) producing a case record for each individual patient; (2) summarizing the data into treatment groups, control groups, or any other meaningful groupings in tabular and graphic forms that show frequency distributions and averages; and (3) conducting appropriate statistical tests to determine the likelihood that results occurred due to chance fluctuations. Moreover, the use of familiar and well-documented statistical techniques is recommended except when novel approaches are absolutely preferable. It should be possible to trace the contribution of an individual patient's raw data to the determination of a probability statement about treatment efficacy.

Communication and Flexibility. In addition to their utility in designing and implementing effective studies of psychotropic agents, the international guidelines emphasize the need for good communication between the investigator and the industry monitor. In fact, close contact between these two entities is as important as well-planned realistic study designs. The guidelines also allow for flexibility of approach, especially for exploratory studies, when such an approach is likely to lead to important clarification of an investigational drug's efficacy or safety, or both.

FDA Regulations

In addition to *recommendations* in the FDA and international guidelines for sound practice in the investigation of the efficacy and safety of new drugs, the FDA has issued formal regulations. These regulations address the obligation of investigators who are responsible for the conduct of the investigation; the obligation of the pharmaceutical companies or other agencies who sponsor the investigation of a new drug; and the obligation of pharmaceutical company monitors, who must supervise certain formal aspects of the investigation. These regulations are currently under revision. Their publication in final form is anticipated in the near future.

These regulations indicate that the protocol for the clinical investigation must be on file with the FDA before the investigation is initiated. The regulations also state that any deviations from the protocol must be reported to the FDA. Both the sponsor and the investigator must provide assurance that the protocol has the approval of the Institutional Review Board for Human Research (IRB) in the responsible institution, hospital, or clinic. Both sponsor and investigator must also provide assurance that the subject has been informed of the nature of the research and that the subject has given his or her written consent for involvement in the proceedings. Any toxic or untoward reaction must be reported promptly. The investigator is required to maintain complete records of all aspects of treatment, including pertinent features of the patient's clinical history, for two years after the approval of the drug for marketing or, if the application is not approved, for two years after the investigation is discontinued.

Through monitors, the sponsor (usually a pharmaceutical company) is responsible for recorded periodic visits to all investigational sites to assure that all explicit and implicit requirements of the protocol are met by the investigator. Monitoring by the sponsor may involve comparing data generated by the investigation with the clinical records of patients involved in the investigation. The obligations of the sponsor, the monitors, and the investigators are numerous and specific (U.S. Department of Health, Education, and Welfare, 1975; 1976; 1977; 1978; 1979). Although these obligations may be of little methodologic or scientific import, they have the *force of law* and can be a part of the assessment of any program of clinical investigation undertaken to support claims of efficacy and safety of new drugs.

The FDA Bioresearch Monitoring Program

In 1977, the FDA adopted an agency-wide Bioresearch Monitoring Program designed to assure the quality and integrity of research data submitted to the agency and to assure the protection of human subjects of clinical trials. This program covers four major areas:
1. Toxicology laboratories that develop the nonclinical data to assure the safety of a product
2. Sponsors and monitors of clinical studies
3. Institutional Review Boards (IRBs) that assure the rights and protection of human subjects in clinical studies
4. Clinical investigators who conduct clinical studies

There are two types of inspections under this program: *surveillance* (data audit) inspections and *directed* ("for cause") inspections. The Clinical Investigations Branch of the Bureau of Drugs currently directs 200 surveillance inspections annually.

When the inspection program was initiated, the clinical investigators selected for inspection were those who had contributed important studies of drugs that were considered promising therapeutic entities or offered important or modest therapeutic gains. However, such selection of "high priority" studies for audit on a routine surveillance basis led to a virtual neglect of certain other types of studies, including studies of drugs of low priority, bioavailability studies, studies by individual noncommercial sponsor-investigators, emergency use studies, studies of over-the-counter drugs, and efficacy studies on certain drugs approved prior to 1962 on the basis of safety only.

In fact, any sample of 200 clinical investigators randomly selected from the printout of some 13,000 currently active clinical investigations would undoubtedly be weighted, for example, with the relatively numerous phase III studies, with studies of low-risk drugs, and with studies with low patient exposure. As a result, a stratified surveillance strategy was developed that embraces all types of drug studies. In the new strategy, however, the extent to which each category is represented in the sample is based on the priority assigned that category. Within this stratification, the selection of the individual studies to be inspected is governed by their significance to the application of which they are a part.

These surveillance inspections are carried out by FDA field investigators, who are supplied with case reports or protocols, or both, as submitted to the agency. In all instances, the investigator is advised in advance of the pending inspection, and a mutually convenient time is selected for the inspection. At the conclusion of the inspection, there is a preliminary discussion of the findings with the investigator.

The FDA investigator's report, or Establishment Investigation Report (EIR), is forwarded to the Division of Scientific Investigations where findings are evaluated to determine the compliance with the regulations and the integrity of the data. The appropriate scientific review division, however, determines whether in light of the inspection findings the study is acceptable in support of efficacy or safety. The Division of Scientific Investigations has adopted the policy of communicating with all clinical investigators visited, even if no serious shortcomings are noted. However, where serious problems are found, a *directed* inspection may be undertaken, usually involving a headquarters scientist. In such cases, written communication with the investigator is delayed until the findings of this second inspection have been evaluated.

Directed inspections may be initiated because of concern by a reviewing medical officer over a study or because of adverse information provided by the sponsor, a patient, or a coworker of the investigator. In view of the deliberations and recommendations of the National Commission for the Protection of Human Subjects of Biomedical and Behavioral Research, studies involving vulnerable subjects, such as the institutionalized mentally infirm are not infrequently subject to Institutional Review Board and/or clinical investigator inspections. Although directed inspections, as well as surveillance inspections, routinely are made with advance warning to the clinical investigator, on rare occasions an unscheduled visit may be deliberately undertaken.

If it appears that an investigator has repeatedly or deliberately failed to comply with the commitments he or she made in becoming a clinical investigator, outlined in Forms FD 1572 and 1573 (U.S. Department of Health, Education, and Welfare, 1975; 1976) or that he or she has submitted false information to a sponsor in Form 1572 or 1573 or in any required report, steps to make the investigator ineligible to undertake investigational drug studies in the future may be initiated. The first step is taken by the Division of Scientific Investigations. This division issues the investigator a letter outlining the deficiencies noted and giving him or her the opportunity to explain these deficiencies either in a letter or at an informal conference. If an explanation is offered and not accepted by the bureau, a recommendation is forwarded to the commissioner that the investigator be offered a regulatory hearing to determine whether he or she is entitled to receive investigational new drugs.

If, following this regulatory hearing, the commissioner determines that the investigator has repeatedly or deliberately failed to comply with conditions of the exempting regulations, has repeatedly or deliberately submittted false information to the sponsor of an investigation, or has failed to furnish adequate assurance that the conditions in the exemption will be met in the future, the commissioner informs the investigator and the sponsor of any investigation in which he or she has been named as a participant that the investigator is not entitled to receive investigational drugs. A statement must also be given to the investigator and his or her sponsors for the basis of this determination.

Once an investigator has been determined ineligible to receive investigational drugs, submissions containing studies by this investigator will be reviewed by the appropriate division. If such studies are determined to be pivotal in determining safety or effectiveness for some therapeutic claim for a marketed drug, approval of a new drug application (NDA) may be withdrawn. In the case of an investigational drug, if the remaining data are inadequate to support a conclusion that it is safe to continue the investigation, the exemption granted by the agency to permit such a study (that is, the investigation of a new drug [IND]) may be terminated unless the sponsor can, in a regulatory hearing, convince the agency that it is safe to continue.

Because disqualification of an investigator may result in a severe penalty to a sponsor, it is appropriate that sponsors receive information of the investigator's unacceptability as expeditiously as is consistent with fairness to the investigator. Unfortunately, disqualification procedures are protracted, and it may be a year or more between the time the agency feels real concern for the activities of the investigator and the time that he or she is eventually declared ineligible to conduct investigational drug studies. During this period the investigator is at liberty to continue ongoing studies or even to contract for new studies unless the privilege to receive investigational drugs is suspended pending the resolution of the disqualification proceeding.

Finally, under current regulations, even when investigators have been disqualified, this information can only be conveyed to sponsors for whom they have done studies. The proposed clinical investigator regulations would permit a somewhat broader dissemination of this information by allowing the commissioner to use discretion in notifying all or any interested persons if it is believed that such notice would further the public interest or promote compliance with the regulations. It is not unreasonable to consider hospital or university administrators or chairs of Institutional Review Boards interested persons. Even under the current regulations, names of all disqualified individuals are available under the Freedom of Information Act.

Results of the FDA Bioresearch Monitoring Program

An analysis has been made of 510 *surveillance* inspection reports received by the Bureau of Drugs between June 1, 1977, and September 30, 1980. In 81 instances, the inspection could not be undertaken for a variety of reasons; for example, the sponsor or the investigator may have chosen not to initiate the study, or the clinical investigator had died or was out of the country. One report contained too little information to be evaluable. Thus 428 reports were evaluable for investigator compliance with FDA regulations.

Of the 428 investigators whose compliance with regulations was evaluable, 79 (19 percent) were found to be in total compliance. However, 29 (7 percent) were found to be so out of compliance that an additional directed inspection was undertaken.

Among the most common deficiencies noted were problems with patient consent (32 percent), inadequate drug accountability (30 percent), no adherence to protocol (17 percent), records inaccuracy (15 percent), and records unavailability (5 percent). Other deficiencies—including the use of concomitant therapy, inappropriate delegation of authority, simultaneous use of more than one investigational drug, and inadequate follow-up of adverse reactions—were found in from 0.2 to 2.6 percent of the reports.

Between June 1, 1977, and September 30, 1980, 139 *directed* ("for cause") inspections were initiated. Of these, 127 have been evaluated to date. From this group, 16 (13 percent) of the investigators have been found ineligible to receive investigational drugs. Severe problems that might lead to disqualification have been found in 27 (21 percent) others.

The Sponsor/Monitor Compliance Program is a special *surveillance* program, which involves inspections of some 50 sponsors and their monitors each year to determine compliance with the *proposed* sponsor/monitor regulations. Between June 1, 1977, and October 1, 1980, 129 of the 165 inspection reports received by the bureau were evaluable. In 68 (53 percent) of the inspections, no significant deviations were noted from the current or proposed regulations with regard to responsibility of sponsors and their monitors. In 61 (47 percent) reports, significant deviations were noted. Among the most frequent deficiencies noted were failure to establish adequacy of laboratory facilities used by the clinical investigator (23 percent), failure to maintain adequate records of drug accountability (23 percent), and absence of standard monitoring procedures (22 percent). A failure to monitor patient records was found in 19 percent of the reports reviewed, and failure to secure Institutional Review Board approval was found in 16 percent. Thirty-one percent of the reports indicated that clinical records had been compared with case reports, while 22 percent of the reports indicated that comparisons had not been undertaken because of company policy.

These problems with evaluation of patient records found in the Sponsor/Monitor Compliance Program are critical. The FDA believes inspection of such records is a pivotal part of monitoring procedures and maintains that case histories should include both case report forms and the underlying raw data. Moreover, there are several reasons why review of the patient's clinical record is undertaken. First, such review helps establish that the patient was a suitable subject for the clinical trial, and that the outcome was as reported. Second, it permits verification of the submitted laboratory data, including EKG and x-ray reports, by comparison with the raw data contained on the original report forms. Third, it helps establish whether or not the patient received unreported concomitant therapy. It is not necessary that the patient be identified by name unless the records of particular individuals require a more detailed study of the cases, or unless there is reason to believe that the records do not represent actual cases studied or do not represent actual results obtained. In such cases, a contact with the subject may be necessary.

How seriously do the faulty studies uncovered in the Bioresearch Monitoring Program affect the validity of the data on which the FDA bases its decisions? Unfortunately, there are no clear-cut answers at this time. The problem is partly one of sampling when both studies and products vary so widely in safety aspects and in significance.

It has been argued that so many clinical investigators are involved in studies of an investigational drug that the poor performance of one or two individuals will make no difference in the overall assessment of the drug's safety or efficacy. However, the FDA's recent experience casts some doubt on this assumption. Since the Bioresearch Monitoring Program was initiated, FDA action on at least two new drug applications has been withheld because of adverse inspectional findings. Pivotal work on an approved new drug application has been found to be invalid, and administrative action has been taken as a result. Investigational exemptions have been terminated in several instances as a result of investigations that revealed false or misleading data in the application.

The FDA has the impression that a high proportion of the directed inspections involve clinical studies of neuropharmacological drug products. This may reflect an active investigational field; an alert reviewing division; or greater difficulties with the design, execution, and monitoring of controlled efficacy studies in this area as compared, for example, with the area of antiinfective or cardiovascular drugs. Of the sixteen investigators declared ineligible to receive investigational drugs since June, 1977, four are psychiatrists while five others conducted trials with neuropharmacological agents. Of twenty-seven cases currently under consideration for disqualification, ten involve neuropharmacological drugs. Six investigators are psychiatrists.

It is difficult to escape the conclusion that many of the serious problems uncovered in the Bioresearch Monitoring Program could have been picked up through better monitoring by sponsors. In some instances, it appears the monitor may have been aware of and may have contributed to some of the observed data manipulations. In other cases, the sponsors have disclosed to the FDA their concern over the investigator's activities as they submitted the study results required by regulations.

Conclusions

Because of sampling variability, unreliability of procedures, vagaries of investigators, and the nature of clinical situations, the results of clinical investigations are not always mutually confirming. Accordingly, programs of replicative studies must be organized and conducted to support a claim of therapeutic efficacy for a new drug. The efficacy of such programs of research is ultimately subject to assessment on some basis or another. Formal provisions for such assessments of programs are a recent development in psychopharmacology, and the structure for such assessments is not complete. Nevertheless, two formal developments may be identified: guidelines for the clinical investigation of new drugs and bioresearch monitoring by the FDA.

The development of guidelines is limited by considerations that limit development of psychopharmacology as well. Among these limiting factors is uncertainty concerning the clinical indications for the optimal use of a psychotropic drug. The FDA and perhaps much of the medical community regard psychiatric drugs as useful for ameliorating certain symptoms in a specified diagnostic category. Inevitably the question arises, "Is the drug effective for a given diagnostic disorder regardless of its symptoms, or effective for a symptom complex regardless of the diagnosis in which it falls?" To some, it seems that a psychotropic drug is a treatment in search of a disease, and to others it seems that the drug modifies certain behaviors and its proper use is not limited to any disease or current diagnosis.

The procedural audits conducted by the FDA in its Bioresearch Monitoring Program as reviewed in this chapter offer no firm conclusions. While the concern generated by this program persists, the intensity of this concern has diminished appreciably. There is now a commonly expressed worry regarding the cumulative effect of burdensome regulations on the American pharmaceutical industry. There is a fear that the psychotropic drugs of the future, as well as most of those of the past, will not be developed in the United States. While it is true that violations of procedural components do arise, it is difficult to determine the significance of these violations. Moreover, some medical investigators see the monitoring program as an unwarranted breach of the confidentiality of the doctor-patient relationship, and other economically minded professionals suspect that this monitoring program is an unnecessarily large and expensive machine to catch a small mouse. The following commentary (Baird, 1980) prepared by a responsible medical officer of a large pharmaceutical company expresses much of the current sentiment.

It is my opinion that if one carefully reviews the regulations which apply to sponsors and monitors, it is very difficult, in theory, to find fault with their intent. When these regulations were discussed two years ago, they were severely criticized by the community of investigators. It could be observed, however, that the FDA has, in essence, codified advices, proposals, and suggestions made by this same investigative community in their speeches, writings, and particularly as members of the FDA Advisory Committees over a period of years. Therefore, these regulations should represent the current state of the art.

From the industry standpoint, there is no doubt that they do impose an enormous burden of expense both in absolute dollars and time. Significant portions of research budgets which are finite are being diverted to meticulously policing and recording of this policing of research projects. It remains to be seen whether this diversion of funds to non-research aspects of investigation will truly return the investment in improved work.

Initially, it was feared that many investigators would prefer not to carry out studies in the face of new regulations with their real and implied sanctions for deviations. To date, this would not seem to be the fact. One of the most contentious aspects of the regulations, at least for the psychopharmacology community two years ago, was the provision that required that access be provided to sponsors and to the FDA to the private records of patients involved in a study. This was perceived as an unwarranted intrusion into the doctor/patient relationship, the patient's personal privacy, etc. It was generally felt that investigators would refuse to provide this access. This has not proved to be a problem.

After two years of experience with these regulations, it remains to be determined whether or not cost/benefit analyses will be positive or negative; that is, will the regulations result in fewer but better industry-sponsored studies or just a reduction in the number of studies sponsored. To date the previously anticipated problems having to do with investigators being unwilling or unable to comply with the proposed FDA regulations have not materialized.

References

Baird, H. L. "Report to the American College of Neuropsychopharmacology." Unpublished report of Sandoz, Inc., 1980.

U.S. Department of Commerce. *Testing Drugs in Anxiety and Depression ACNP-FDA Guidelines Materials.* NTIS PB-276-728. Springfield, Va.: National Technical Information Service, 1977.

U.S. Department of Health, Education, and Welfare, Food and Drug Administration. *Statement of Investigator.* Form FD 1573. Rockville, Md.: Food and Drug Administration, 1975.

U.S. Department of Health, Education, and Welfare, Food and Drug Administration. *Statement of Investigator (Clinical Pharmacology).* Form FD 1572. Rockville, Md.: Food and Drug Administration, 1976.

U.S. Department of Health, Education, and Welfare, Food and Drug Administration. "Clinical Investigations: Proposed Establishment of Regulations and Obligations of Sponsors and Monitors." *Federal Register,* Part IV, September 27, 1977, *42,*(187), Part IV.

U.S. Department of Health, Education, and Welfare, Food and Drug Administration. *Guidelines for the Clinical Evaluation of Antidepressant Drugs.* HEW (FDS) 77-3042. Rockville, Md.: Food and Drug Administration, 1977a.

U.S. Department of Health, Education, and Welfare, Food and Drug Administration. "Obligations of Clinical Investigators of Regulated Articles: Proposed Establishment of Regulations." *Federal Register,* August 8, 1978, *43*(153), Part V.

U.S. Department of Health, Education, and Welfare, Food and Drug Administration. *Notice of Claimed Investigational Exemption for a New Drug.* Form FD 1571. Rockville, Md.: Food and Drug Administration, 1979.

U.S. Department of Health, Education, and Welfare, Food and Drug Administration. *Guidelines for Clinical Evaluation of Psychoactive Drugs in Infants and Children.* HEW (FDA) 79-3055. Rockville, Md.: Food and Drug Administration, 1979a.

Wittenborn, J. R. "Guidelines for Clinical Trials of Psychotropic Drugs." In J. R. Wittenborn (Ed.), *Pharmakopyshciatrie Neuro-Psychopharmakologie.* Munich: Verlag Dokumentation, 1977.

J. R. Wittenborn is university professor of psychology and education and director of the Interdisciplinary Research Center, Rutgers University. He was president of the American College of Neuropsychopharmacology in 1973 and has been actively involved in the development of guidelines for conducting clinical psychopharmacological research.

Frances O. Kelsey is director of the Division of Scientific Investigations of the Bureau of Drugs. She is responsible for monitoring the activities of those involved in the testing of drugs for clinical use.

*There is room for improvement in remedial training
programs. Sound assessment holds out a hope for
more evident success.*

Evaluating and Improving Remedial Training Programs

Dan Baugher

Over the past twelve years we have witnessed a widening interest in remedial training programs for the "disadvantaged" (Goodman and others,
1973; Kirchner and Lucas, 1971; Watson and Rowe, 1976). In general, these
programs evolved as a consequence of community pressure—pressure for
industry to increase its development and hiring of individuals with limited
educational and work experience (Gustafson, 1973). For example, remedial
training is often provided to workers selected to meet Equal Employment
Opportunity (EEO) goals in order to compensate for their "restricted"
backgrounds.

    Unfortunately, however, the impact of these training programs on
the individuals participating in them and the organizations sponsoring
them has not been adequately documented. No general review of their success or failure has been published. Yet remedial programs involve many
hours of training as well as susbstantial cost. In fact, these programs and
studies of their success provide vivid examples of some of the most basic
problems facing the evaluation of various training programs in industry
today.

    It is the purpose of this chapter to shed light on the remedial train-
ing process through a thorough review of the literature. At the same time,

D. Baugher (Ed.). *New Directions for Program Evaluation: Measuring Effectiveness*, no. 11.
San Francisco: Jossey-Bass, September 1981

the reader will recognize that the conceptual and methodological problems found in remedial efforts often appear in other types of training as well. Many of the suggestions for improvement offered at the end of this chapter can help training evaluators and implementors in the other circumstances.

In reviewing the literature, three questions were asked. First, are the studies conceptually and methodologically sound? Second, from the available evidence, do remedial training programs meet their stated objectives? In other words, do trainees attain greater academic and work skills, gain improved work and social attitudes, or perform better? Third, given the present state of the art, can anything be done to improve the training-evaluation process?

Although this chapter reviews the bulk of the scientific studies conducted on remedial training over the past twelve years, few of these studies have a tight conceptual framework or clear, precise objectives. Often evaluators fail to recognize the methodological problems inherent in their studies and, as a result, the value of their efforts is hard to interpret. In general these problems in evaluation can be broadly classified into either design or measurement problems.

Design Problems

The evaluation of remedial efforts is often conducted in the field. Because of the field setting, certain design problems are frequently inevitable. Others are avoidable.

The Presumption of Experimental Design. The most frequent problem in the evaluation of remedial training programs is the implicit assumption of an experimental outcome even though the program lacks the necessary control or comparison group. This is not to say that the experimental approach to the evaluation of training programs is absolutely necessary. Rather, the problem in these studies is the presumption of, not the necessity of, an experimental design. Trainees are subjected to a variety of treatments such as remedial education or skills training before putting them on the job; a follow-up is then done to determine their success or failure. Should this group succeed, it is concluded that the program worked; if the group fails, it is concluded that the program failed. While these educated guesses about the causal relation of the program to trainee success may be correct, it is also possible to conclude that the special treatment had absolutely nothing to do with trainee success on the job (Gustafson, 1973).

High Attrition Rates. The substantial attrition found in many remedial training programs makes it difficult to assess the exact influence of the programs. In some cases, less than 60 percent of those beginning the training finish. Further, if these trainees are found to be successful on the job, it is often concluded that the training procedures worked. Yet it is perhaps more likely that the program simply acted as a screening device (albeit, an expensive one) to identify those who were able to complete training (Gordon and Scott, 1972). Such determination is likely to make trainees appear successful when later working on the job, especially if the criterion of job performance is turnover or absenteeism.

Potential Practice Effects. Evaluators of remedial efforts rarely design studies that assess the effects of practice on the scores achieved by trainees on skills tests or scholastic tests. This lack makes it difficult to determine whether the gains found in these areas are due to practice or training. This problem is most acute in those studies that do not make it clear whether trainees took alternate forms of the same test before and after training or the same form. In either case, practice can contribute to any gains found; in those instances where the same form is used, trainees may gain even more as a result of their familiarity with the questions. Ultimately, this design problem can be quite critical since it is unlikely that gains made on these tests, as a consequence of practice, will generalize to other different measures of the same capacity. In short, the gains, though statistically significant, may not be real.

Problems with Matched Controls. Some studies of remedial training attempt to make comparisons between training graduates and another set of workers selected for their similarity to trainees. In these studies differences between the two groups are assumed to be due to the training effort. While this attempt at matching may be of some use, it is far from perfect. First, the matching of these two groups after the training effort (that is, ex post facto design) makes it impossible to rule out differences between the two groups due to self-selection. In other words, the two groups may be different as a consequence of uncontrollable factors (for example, motivation), leading one to be in the training group and the other to be in the so called control group. Second, it is obviously impossible to control for all relevant variables in the matching process, not only because of practical difficulties, but also because of our limited knowledge of which extraneous variables are potentially biasing. Third, the nonequivalence of the two groups may lead the training effort to look worse than it is as a consequence of regression artifacts (Campbell and Erlebacher, 1970).

Subject Incomparability. It is difficult to describe precisely the characteristics of trainees participating in remedial training programs because of lack of information. However, a general characterization would be as follows: Trainees are usually members of a minority group, not regular members of the work force, often under twenty-two years of age, and of a poverty level specified by the Department of Labor. Of course, variations from this characterization do occur in some studies and make it difficult to derive a generalizable statement regarding the efficacy of certain remedial approaches.

Measurement Problems

In addition to the design problems listed above, studies of remedial training are subject to a variety of measurement problems. The source of these problems is the rather haphazard selection of criterion measures of training efficacy. As has been true for many other program assessments, measurement in the evaluation of remedial training has followed the principle of "take what is readily available."

Grade-Equivalent Scores. One consequence of this approach is the selection of grade-equivalent scores to assess the gains of trainees on certain intellectual and skills measures. Yet these scores may be misleading under certain circumstances. Like a number of derived scores, the units of measurement of grade-equivalent scores (that is, tenths of a grade) do not represent reasonably equivalent amounts of the subject matter being measured (Davis, 1964, p. 40). As such, grade-equivalent scores may distort the amount of improvement attained by a student or group depending on the particular pre- and post-training raw scores achieved. Movement from one grade-equivalent score to another often depends on the score's initial location on the continuum. A specific gain in the number of items answered correctly may lead to a statistically significant gain at one point on the grade-equivalent continuum but not at another point. In short, the statistical analysis of grade-equivalent scores is hard to interpret because these scores give us little information about the number of items answered correctly and the student's absolute level of mastery.

In addition, *none* of the studies indicates what grade level on the criterion measures is sufficient to enable trainees to master their future job positions. Improvements in grade level consequently say little about the real success of the training programs. Significant gains can be achieved even though no trainee reaches the necesary "passing" score for successful work.

Nonequivalence of Criterion Measures. To simplify their work, evaluators of remedial training often use turnover and supervisor ratings as measures of the success of their efforts. Unfortunately, the meaning of these measures for graduates of remedial training may be different from the meaning for the general work force.

In the case of turnover, it is possible that those graduates of remedial programs who leave a company are leaving for a better position than that normally afforded to them after training at their present company. In this case, high turnover in graduates of remedial training may be taken as an indication that the effort worked better than expected in teaching graduates relevant job skills. Evaluators who use turnover as a measure of training efficacy should recognize that turnover can have both positive and negative connotations as well as many different causes (Dalton and Todor, 1979).

Supervisor ratings are also equivocal measures of success. It is hard to predict whether supervisors will treat these graduates differently from ordinary workers. Nonetheless, it is not uncommon for criterion measurements based on ratings (rather than more objective observations) to possess some kind of bias. A good example is sex bias in school grades: Teachers generally give slightly lower grades to boys than to girls even when both have identical objective scholastic scores (Jensen, 1980, p. 383). If supervisors view this special group of workers differently from the general work force, they may treat them more harshly and thus make the training effort look bad. In contrast, of course, they may be more lenient as a consequence of political pressures and, in turn, cause the program to look good. In either case, the efficacy of the training effort remains obscure.

Presumption of Job-Relatedness in Post-Training Measures. In some instances, evaluators of remedial efforts presume the job-relatedness of their post-training measures. Higher scores at the end of training are thought to imply that graduates will perform better on the job than they would have at the beginning of training. Caution in making this prediction is needed. In the case of clerical or typing tests, the apparent content validity of the measures may be sufficient to enable such a prediction. Nonetheless, if the post-training measure has no obvious job-related validity, such a prediction is clearly out of line. Particularly questionable are predictions of future job success from gains in instruments measuring intellectual, personal, and social skills. Yet most of the studies in this review seem to presume, at least implicitly, the job-relatedness of gains in these areas even though evidence for their relevance is sparse and inconsistent (Beatty, 1975; Gavin and Toole, 1973; Kirkpatrick and others, 1968).

Differential Validity of Ability Measures. In comparison to the measurement problems discussed so far, questions of differential validity are relatively minor in assessing the efficacy of remedial training. Differential validity arises when a particular measure of ability is related to job success in the general work force but not specifically to success in the minority subset under consideration (for example, disadvantaged workers). As a consequence, higher scores on this measure at the end of remedial training may not imply higher job performance in the future. The controversy over test bias is complicated, and reviews of test validation research with respect to differential validity show inconsistencies (Schmidt and others, 1973; Schmidt and Hunter, 1974). Some writers feel that true differential validity rarely exists (Bray and Moses, 1972; Humphreys, 1973; Jensen, 1980). Evaluators of remedial training programs should become familiar with this issue so that they can consider its implications (if any) for their studies of training efficacy. (See Jensen, 1980, pp. 367–463, for a thorough discussion of test bias and Heath, 1979, for an examination of how differential validity in IQ tests may cause compensatory education programs to appear ineffective.)

Meeting Stated Objectives

Deciding whether remedial training programs have met their stated objectives is a difficult task, to say the least. Nonetheless, the most robust and logically consistent effects of remedial efforts are reported in this section.

Academic Skills. Remedial training often stresses instruction in basic academic skills and attempts to upgrade the reading and arithmetic abilities of "disadvantaged" workers (Burck, 1968; Gassler, 1967; Janger, 1969). From this review, it appears that remedial training programs, lasting an average of 300 hours, produce mean gains of about one to three grade levels in these areas (Beatty, 1975; Campbell, 1969; Gavin and Toole, 1973; Gordon and others, 1974; Hinrichs, 1972; Mollenkopf, 1969). These gains are found in a diversity of organizations including Proctor and Gamble, Inland Steel, and IBM. Unfortunately, significant gains seem more difficult to obtain for remedial trainees who have not graduated from high school than for those who have graduated (Campbell, 1969; Patten and Clark, 1968). Also, arithmetic skills, especially arithmetic computation, are easier to increase than verbal skills (Beatty, 1975; Campbell, 1969; Gavin and Toole, 1973; Hinrichs, 1972; Mollenkopf, 1969).

Job Skills. The development of job skills is cited by numerous investigators as an important goal for remediation training (Chernick and Smith, 1969; Main, 1968; Schenkel and Hudson, 1970; Scott, 1970; Solie, 1968; Stromsdorfer, 1968). In this situation, some investigators use the number of trainees placed on the job as a measure of job skill development (Kirchner and Lucas, 1972; Schenkel and Hudson, 1970; Watson and Rowe, 1976). Unfortunately, mere placement on a job says little about the skills obtained by a trainee. Other investigators have used the labor market experiences of graduates as a measure of their skills acquisition (Main, 1968; Solie, 1968; Stromsdorfer, 1968). Yet labor market outcomes are a very gross measure of graduate experiences, influenced by many biasing factors. (I am not questioning labor market experience as an important measure but rather its proposed relation to obtaining job skills.) It is quite possible, for instance, that when graduates show better labor market experiences than "matched" controls the difference is due more to the special job placement often afforded graduates than to the special training.

Fortunately, remedial training programs fostering clerical skills development have benefited from clearer evaluation. Substantial gains can be made in the areas of filing, spelling, and grammatical expression in as little as sixty hours (Beatty, 1975; Mollenkopf, 1969). Moreover, post-training filing ability appears to be related to two-year job performance (but not two-year earnings) (Beatty, 1975).

Personal and Social Variables. One finds among the stated objectives of remedial efforts a variety of goals related to the restoration of trainees to the mainstream of society (Gordon and Scott, 1972). Consequently, the modification of personal and social variables, including the "self-development" of trainees, appears to be an important goal for certain programs. Regrettably, little energy has been devoted to the validation of efforts directed at social integration. Articles abound with anecdotes concerning dramatic changes in the lives of trainees, but systematic analyses of the effects of training on personal, social, and motivational dimensions do not clearly substantiate the efficacy of training in these areas (Allerhand and others, 1969; Goodale, 1971; Frank, 1969). Among those studies that report concrete data, findings about the effect of training on these variables are inconsistent (Beatty, 1975; Gordon and Scott, 1972).

Job Turnover. The unusually high turnover rates (for example, 45-65 percent) frequently found among disadvantaged workers (Campbell, 1969; Ferman, 1968; Purcell and Cavanaugh, 1972; Ross and Wheeler, 1971) are rarely reduced through remediation training (Goodman and others, 1973; Triandis and others, 1974). Some authors suggest that remedial training actually may foster *increased* job dissatisfaction and turnover by raising the job expectations of trainees beyond the realities of the work setting (Goodman and others, 1973; Quinn and others, 1970; Triandis and others, 1974). One study of disadvantaged workers placed under sensitivity-trained supervisors lends support to this notion; trained workers exhibited a higher turnover (80 percent) than untrained workers (45 percent) (Farr, 1969).

Many other factors, which are quite independent of the training experience, appear to influence the job retention of disadvantaged workers. The nature of their jobs (Allerhand and others, 1969; Goodman, 1969; Janger, 1972; Lipsky and others, 1971; Quinn and others, 1970; Shlensky, 1970) and their ages and degree of family responsibility (Gurin, 1968; Hinrichs, 1972; Kirchner and Lucas; 1972; Lipsky and others, 1971; Quinn and others, 1970; Rosen, 1969; Shlensky, 1970) are prime examples of influential variables affecting disadvantaged worker retention.

Job Performance Ratings. Job performance ratings are occasionally used to validate the effectiveness of remedial training programs. It seems from these studies that graduates of skills-oriented remedial training programs receive, at least eventually, more positive ratings on work-related items than regular hires who receive no training (Beatty, 1975; Gustafson, 1973). In contrast, no difference in the performance ratings of remedial trainees (who completed a company orientation program) and matched direct hires is reported by Quinn and others (1970), although the attitudes of trainees seemed to be more positive toward their work.

Still, these results cannot be generalized to all types of training (for example, academic development). More important, such factors as differential treatment of trainees on the job, biased supervisor ratings, or motivational differences between trainees and the comparison groups—not training—may account for the reported outcomes.

Objective Performance Measures. Direct measurement of the quantity and quality of individual job performance is rare in industry and difficult to obtain under the best of circumstances. Nonetheless, Gustafson (1973) presents a study in which the quantity of work produced by remedial training graduates is assessed on their jobs as directory assistance telephone operators. In a comparison of this group to matched direct hires, he finds no difference in productivity curves after thirteen months of assessments. Still, it is not clear why anyone would expect this program to foster major differences in job proficiency in the first place. Instruction was provided in basic educational subjects and other topics such as personal hygiene and not in the job-related behaviors necessary for performance as a telephone operator.

Improving the Training-Evaluation Process

Perhaps the most significant flaw in the implementation and evaluation of remedial training programs is the almost total absence of any guiding theoretical or conceptual framework. Disadvantaged workers are given training to develop their mathematical and reading skills, yet there is no preliminary attempt to gain evidence that the skills are needed in their future job positions. Attempts to develop certain attitudinal and social variables are initiated, but these are neither theoretically nor empirically justified. Even when seemingly important job skills are emphasized, the evaluation of the training program is usually quite weak.

Requirements for the administration of a successful remedial training program are discussed below. These requirements provide a guiding framework useful in the development and assessment of remedial efforts. This framework may also be generalizable to other types of training. Many human development programs suffer similar problems (Catalanello and Kirkpatrick, 1968; Owen and Croll, 1974; Porras and Berg, 1978) and desperately need some sort of conceptual model (Snyder and others, 1980).

Determining Training Needs and Objectives. As a first step, implementors of remedial training must identify the specific development needs of disadvantaged workers participating in *their* programs. No general training program can be suggested for different groups of workers. The program will vary from company to company depending upon organizational and job requirements and trainee deficits. In addition, value-laden assumptions about the job-related deficiencies of disadvantaged workers must be avoided. While it is true, for example, that many disadvantaged workers suffer educational deficits, these deficits, though socially undesirable, do not necessarily make them unsuitable for work in certain entry-level positions.

Fortunately, there are a number of useful approaches for determining the training needs of workers. As a starting point, implementors of remedial efforts can use job analyses of positions for which the disadvantaged workers are scheduled to enter. These job analyses should be behavioral in nature and enable trainers to determine exactly what trainees should be able to do upon completion of a remedial program (O'Reilly, 1973; Schneier, 1974, 1976). If job analyses are not available, trainers may attempt to develop their own. (See McCormick, 1976, for a detailed investigation of job analysis.) Next, training implementors may actively solicit ideas from managers and employees regarding the training needs of disadvantaged workers (Berger, 1976). Finally, disadvantaged trainees may be permitted to perform on their future jobs for a short period of time. This performance should allow trainers to assess their job-related deficiencies. No matter which approach is used, a concrete set of behaviorally oriented learning objectives must emerge for the remedial effort (Gustafson, 1973; Rundquist, 1972).

It might also be wise for organizations that hire the disadvantaged to consider alternatives to training, such as job redesign. If, for example, the major obstacles to the success of trainees is a training or work manual requiring twelfth-grade reading skills, it may make more sense to modify the manual than to try and make up for a lifetime of educational disadvantage through remedial training.

Designing and Implementing a Training Program. After the objectives of a training program are determined, many important questions remain. At this point, training implementors typically give considerable attention to the questions of training method, program length, and trainer selection. (These issues are not considered in this section; see Hinrichs, 1976, for a thorough discussion of them.) At the same time, however, the question of program evaluation is usually given very little attention. Trainers often talk about evaluation, but few give it a central role in the design and implementation of their programs (Dvorkin, 1972; Wirtz and Goldstein, 1975). The same appears to be true for remedial efforts. With some notable exceptions, the studies reviewed in this chapter appear to be relatively unplanned attempts at program evaluation.

It is not surprising that substantial resistance exists to the evaluation of remedial training programs (and other programs as well). Budgets must be justified continually, especially in the United States government, and evaluation can be an intimidating component in this constant battle for funds (Campbell, 1979). In addition, the narrow role often assigned to evaluation fosters the belief in trainers that they will be either "right" or "wrong" following an assessment of their efforts.

Implementors of remedial training must recognize that the evaluation of a program provides critical feedback to them as well as to the organization. More specifically, they must ensure that the methods for evaluating their efforts are recognized and planned for early. The administrative functions of training and evaluation should work together in this process, not separately (Campbell, 1979). In this way, problems of measurement and experimental design can be minimized. There are times when a program's evaluation may be planned post hoc, but this approach is usually not preferable. When evaluation planning happens after the fact, multidimensional scaling techniques may help pinpoint the goals of an ongoing program and provide a framework for discussion (Fernandez, 1979).

Top management must understand that evaluation is not an "all or none" assessment. If the goals of training are justified in the first place, a negative evaluation of a program's present efforts should not be taken as a rationale for ending the program. Without this kind of perspective, evaluation is likely to continue taking a back seat in the planning of remedial training programs.

Evaluating Training. There is probably no single general measure of effectiveness applicable to any complex system such as training (Connolly and Deutsch, 1980). A case in point is the fact that many factions have an interest in the outcomes of remedial efforts. Each of these factions (for example, line managers versus the accounting department) typically have different views of what constitutes program effectiveness. As a result, implementors of remedial training must attempt to select a comprehensive set of measures that reflect the potential interests of the organizational constituencies concerned with their efforts. The selection might include measures of job behavior, job satisfaction, rate of promotion, changes in salaries, turnover, cost benefit and (for government programs) labor market experiences (Ashenfelter, 1978). The interpretation and measurement of each of these outcomes will pose different problems. It is not impossible for a program to score high on one measure and low on another. A program that fosters a large number of behavioral changes may take substantial time, for instance, and not rate well on measures of cost benefit.

In addition to striving for comprehensiveness in their assessment, training implementors must ensure that the specific measures chosen are timely, meaningful, and as free from random error and bias as possible (Hersey, 1979). No perfect measure exists, but awareness of potential problems early in the planning stage may help considerably in the final analysis. Measurements of relevant variables should be taken as the program progresses and not just at the end (Goldstein, 1978) so that corrective action can be taken if something appears to be going wrong. Finally, the qualitative experiences of trainers, trainees, and management may also be of some use in assessing the program although they are often difficult to quantify (Campbell, 1979).

After a set of measures is selected, a statistical design for determining the causal relationship of the remedial effort to changes in these measures must be chosen. This is the point at which very subtle statistical problems may arise. For example, statistical adjustment to partial-out pretest differences between a "control" group and trainees, commonly used in remedial efforts, may really underestimate the impact of the effort (Campbell, 1979).

It is ironic that the hallmark of experimental design, random assignment of subjects to conditions, may also create inferential problems. Randomness may upset the natural assignment of trainees to training, making the design a treatment itself or at least making it difficult to generalize the results of the study to the real training environment (Bryk, 1978). In addition, the emphasis on mean differences, prominent in this approach, may obscure important changes in variability created by an apparently successful program. If the goal is to cause trainees to meet some set level of achievement or "passing" score, an increase in the variability of the scores may cause more workers to fail even though the group does better, on the average, following training (Bryk, 1978).

One design that holds promise for programs that have measurements of relevant variables prior to the actual training program is the interrupted time-series design. This design involves the measurement of relevant variables a number of times before and after training. If some change occurs after training, which is different from the normal fluctuations apparent prior to training, there is a strong chance that training is the cause. If a comparison group can be added to this design to detect possible environmental contaminations, the design will work even better; however, the comparison group is not necessary. Such a design lends itself to remedial efforts when trainees have already worked for the company. In this case, performance evaluations or behavioral assessments could be taken for the group on a number of occasions before and after training. This approach will also work quite well for government-sponsored programs in which worker salary after training is important, since the salary of trainees in the years prior to training usually can be obtained rather easily.

Another design that may help implementors of remedial efforts determine their ability to meet program objectives in the face of critical time constraints is Program Evaluation and Review Technique (PERT). PERT analysis can show where the remedial effort is the slowest (that is, the critical path) and suggest potential changes in the program that could save time (Klosterman, 1979).

Conclusions

The most discouraging finding of the review described in this chapter is the lack of planning apparent in the design and evaluation of remedial training programs. The available data suggest that training can produce average gains of about one to three grade levels in the reading and arithmetic skills of disadvantaged workers, but these skills are not clearly related to trainee performance on the job. Training in clerical skills appears effective, but studies of skills acquisition in other areas are unconvincing. Furthermore, the personal and social skills of disadvantaged workers do not show substantial improvement. In contrast, performance ratings show improvement although research on the objective performance of trainees and job turnover does not show any gains.

Nonetheless, the implementation and evaluation of remedial efforts is not a hopeless task. The framework presented in this chapter emphasizes the need for advance planning. If the steps outlined are put into practice, improvement in the remedial training process should become apparent. Administrators who are interested in setting up a program to assess the effects of training on job behaviors may consult "A Guide to the Participant Action Approach," produced by the United States Office of Personnel Management (1980), for further information. In addition, Rossi, Freeman, and Wright (1979) present an introduction to quasi-experimental designs, such as the interrupted time series, which are often useful in assessing the efficacy of training efforts. A more detailed analysis of this subject can be found in Cook and Campbell (1979).

References

Allerhand, M. E., Friedlander, F., Malone, J. E., Medow, H., and Rosenberg, M. *A Study of the Impact and Effectiveness of the Comprehensive Manpower Project of Cleveland (AIM-JOBS)*. Office of Policy, Evaluation, and Research, U.S. Department of Labor, Contract No. 41-7-002-37, Cleveland, Ohio: Case Western Reserve University, Cleveland College, and AIM Research Project, December, 1969.

Ashenfelter, O. "Estimating the Effect of Training Programs on Earnings." *The Review of Economics and Statistics*, 1978, *60*(1), 47-57.

Beatty, R. W. "A Two-Year Study of Hard-Core Unemployed Clerical Workers: Effects of Scholastic Achievement, Clerical Skills, and Self-Esteem on Job Success." *Personnel Psychology*, 1975, *28*, 165-173.

Berger, L. "A Dew Line for Training and Development: The Needs Analysis Survey." *The Personnel Administrator*, November, 1976, pp. 51-55.

Bray, D. W., and Moses, J. L. "Personnel Selection." *Annual Review of Psychology*, 1972, *23*, 545-576.

Bryk, A. S. "Evaluating Program Impact: A Time to Cast Away Stones, A Time to Gather Stones Together." In S. B. Anderson and C. D. Coles (Eds.), *New Directions for Program Evaluation: Exploring Purposes and Dimensions*, no. 1. San Francisco: Jossey-Bass, 1978.

Burck, G. "A New Business for Business: Reclaiming Human Resources." *Fortune*, 1968, *77*, 159-161.

Campbell, D. "Assessing the Impact of Planned Social Change." *Evaluation and Program Planning*, 1979, *2*, 67-90.

Campbell, D. T., and Erlebacher, A. E. "How Regression Artifacts in Quasi-Experimental Evaluations Can Mistakenly Make Compensatory Education Look Harmful." In J. Hellmuth (Ed.), *Disadvantaged Child*. Vol. 3: *Compensatory Education: A National Debate*. New York: Brunner/Mazel, 1970.

Campbell, R. "Employing the Disadvantaged: Inland Steel's Experience." *Issues and Industrial Society*, 1969, *1*, 30–42.

Catalanello, R., and Kirkpatrick, D. "Evaluating Training Programs." *Training and Development Journal*, 1968, *22*(5), 2–9.

Chernick, J., and Smith, G. "Employing the Disadvantaged." In P. B. Doeringer (Ed.), *Programs to Employ the Disadvantaged*. Englewood Cliffs, N.J.: Prentice-Hall, 1969.

Connolly, T., and Deutsch, S. J. "Performance Measurement: Some Conceptual Issues." *Evaluation and Program Planning*, 1980, *3*, 35–43.

Cook, T. D., and Campbell, D. T. *Quasi-Experimentation: Design and Analysis Issues for Field Settings*. Chicago: Rand McNally, 1979.

Dalton, D. R., and Todor, W. D. "Turnover Turned Over: An Expanded and Positive Perspective." *Academy of Management Review*, 1979, *4*(2), 223–235.

Davis, F. B. *Educational Measurements and Their Interpretations*. Belmont, Calif.: Wadsworth, 1964.

Dvorkin, R. S. "Evaluation of Training." In J. Famularo (Ed.), *Handbook of Modern Personnel Administration*. New York: McGraw-Hill, 1972.

Farr, J. L. "Industrial Training Programs for Hard-Core Unemployed." Paper presented at 17th annual workshop in industrial psychology (Division 14) of the American Psychological Association, Washington, D.C., Aug. 1969.

Ferman, L. A. *The Negro and Equal Employment Opportunities*. New York: Praeger, 1968.

Fernandez, D. "*Post Hoc* Procedures for Planning and Evaluation." *Evaluation and Program Planning*, 1979, *2*, 219–222.

Frank, H. H. "On the Job Training for Minorities: An Internal Study." Unpublished doctoral dissertation, University of California, Los Angeles, 1969.

Gassler, E., "How Companies Are Helping the Uneducated Worker." *Personnel*, 1967, *44*, 47–55.

Gavin, J. F., and Toole, D. L. "Validity of Aptitude Tests for the 'Hardcore Unemployed.'" *Personnel Psychology*, 1973, *26*, 139–146.

Goldstein, I. L. "The Pursuit of Validity in the Evaluation of Training Programs." *Human Factors*, 1978, *20*, 131–144.

Goodale, J. G. "Background Characteristics, Orientation, Work Experience, and Work Values of Employees Hired from Human Resources Development Applicants by Companies Affiliated with the National Alliance of Businessmen." Unpublished doctoral dissertation, Bowling Green State University, 1971.

Goodman, P. S. "Hiring, Training, and Retaining the Hard-Core." *Industrial Relations*, 1969, *9*, 54–66.

Goodman, P. S., Paransky, H., and Salipante, P. "Hiring, Training, and Retaining the Hard-Core Unemployed: A Selected Review." *Journal of Applied Psychology*, 1973, *58*, 23–33.

Gordon, M. E., and Scott, R. D. "Evaluation of a Manpower Development Project in Terms of Its Effects on the Personal Lives of Its Graduates." *Journal of Vocational Behavior*, 1972, *2*, 467–478.

Gordon, M. E., Arvey, R. D., Daffron, W. C., and Umberger, D. L. "Racial Differences in the Impact of Mathematics Training at a Manpower Development Program." *Journal of Applied Psychology*, 1974, *59*, 253–258.

Gurin, G. *Inner City Youth in a Job Training Project*. Ann Arbor: University of Michigan, Institute for Social Research, 1968.

Gustafson, H. W. "Special Treatment for Special People: A Minority Report of the Training of Minorities." *Business Perspectives*, 1973, *9*, 1-11.

Heath, L. "Differential Validity: Another Threat to Compensatory Education Evaluations." *Evaluation and Program Planning*, 1979 *2*, 25-32.

Hersey, J. C. "'Dirty' Research in 'Real' Places: A Practitioner's Guide to Program Evaluation in the Human Services." *Evaluation and Program Planning*, 1979, *2*, 153-157.

Hinrichs, J. R. "Evaluation of an Industrial Training Program for the Hard-Core." *Proceedings of the 80th Annual Convention of the American Psychological Association*, 1972, *7*, 445-446.

Hinrichs, J. R. "Personnel Training." In M. Dunnette (Ed.), *Handbook of Industrial and Organizational Psychology*. Chicago: Rand McNally, 1976.

Humphreys, L. G. "Statistical Definitions of Test Validity for Minority Groups." *Journal of Applied Psychology*, 1973, *58*, 1-4.

Janger, A. "New Start for the Harder Hard-Core." *The Conference Board Record*, 1969, *6*, 10-20.

Janger, A. *Employing the Disadvantaged: A Company Perspective*. New York: The Conference Board, 1972.

Jensen, A. R. *Bias in Mental Testing*. New York: Free Press, 1980.

Kirchner, W., and Lucas, J. "Some Research on Motivating the Hard-Core." *Training in Business and Industry*, 1971, *8*, 30-31.

Kirchner, W., and Lucas, J. "The Hard-Core in Training—Who Makes It?" *Training and Development Journal*, 1972, *26*, 34-38.

Kirkpatrick, J. J., Ewen, R. B., Barrett, R. S., and Katzell, R. A. *Testing and Fair Employment*. New York: New York University Press, 1968.

Klosterman, D. F. "The Application of PERT in Evaluation of Human Service Programs." *Evaluation and Program Planning*, 1979, *2*, 59-66.

Lipsky, D., Drotning, J., and Fottler, M. "Some Correlates of Training Success in a Coupled On-The-Job Training Program." *The Quarterly Review of Economics and Business*, 1971, *11*, 41-61.

Main, E. D. "A Nationwide Evaluation of M.D.T.A. Institutional Job Training." *Journal of Human Resources*, 1968, *3*, 159-170.

McCormick, E. J. "Job and Task Analysis." In M. Dunnette (Ed.), *Handbook of Industrial and Organizational Psychology*. Chicago: Rand McNally, 1976.

Mollenkopf, W. G. "Some Results of Three Basic Skills Training Programs in an Industrial Setting. *Journal of Applied Psychology*, 1969, *53*, 343-347.

O'Reilly, A. "What Value Is Job Analysis in Training?" *Personnel Review* (Great Britain), 1973, *2* (3), 50-60.

Owen, W. B., and Croll, P. R. *Productivity Enhancement Efforts in the Federal Government: A Report of Survey Results, Program Report Evaluation, and Implications for Research*. Personnel Research Report No. 74-1. Washington, D.C.: U.S. Civil Service Commission, Personnel Research and Development Center, 1974.

Patten, T. H., and Clark, G. "Literacy Training and Job Placement of Hard-Core Unemployed Negroes in Detroit." *Journal of Human Resources*, 1968, *3*, 25-46.

Porras, J. E., and Berg, P. O. "The Impact of Organizational Development." *Academy of Management Review*, 1978, *3*, 249-266.

Purcell, T. V., and Cavanaugh, G. F. *Blacks in the Industrial World: Issues for the Manager*. New York: Free Press, 1972.

Quinn, R., Fine, B., and Levitin, T. *Turnover and Training: A Social Psychological Study of Disadvantaged Workers.* Ann Arbor: Survey Research Center, University of Michigan, 1970.

Rosen, H. *A Group Orientation Approach for Facilitating the Work Adjustment of the Hard-Core Unemployed.* Final Report, U.S. Department of Labor Washington, D.C.: U.S. Government Printing Office, 1969.

Ross, J. C., and Wheeler, R. H. *Black Belonging.* Westport, Conn.: Greenwood Press, 1971.

Rossi, P. H., Freeman, H. E., and Wright, S. R. *Evaluation: A Systematic Approach.* Beverly Hills, Calif.: Sage Publications, 1979.

Rundquist, E. "Designing and Improving Job Training Courses." *Personnel Psychology,* 1972, *25* (1), 41–52.

Schenkel, K. F., and Hudson, R. H. "Reclaiming the Hard-Core Unemployed Through Training." *Professional Psychology,* 1970, *1,* 439–443.

Schmidt, F. L., Berner, J. C., and Hunter, J. E. "Racial Difference in Validity of Employment Tests: Reality or Illusion?" *Journal of Applied Psychology,* 1973, *58,* 5–9.

Schmidt, F. L., and Hunter, J. E. "Racial and Ethnic Bias in Psychological Tests: Divergent Implications of Two Definitions of Test Bias." *American Psychologist,* 1974, *29,* 1–8.

Schneier, C. E. "Training and Development Programs: What Learning Theory and Research Have to Offer." *Personnel Journal,* 1974, *53,* 288–293, 300.

Schneier, C. E. "Content Validity: The Necessity of a Behavioral Job Description." *The Personnel Administrator,* February, 1976, *21* (2), 38–44.

Scott, L. C. "The Economic Effectiveness of On-The-Job Training: The Experience of the Bureau of Indian Affairs in Oklahoma. *Industrial and Labor Relations Review,* 1970, *23,* 220–236.

Shlensky, B. "Determinants of Turnover in NABS-JOBS Programs to Employ the Disadvantaged." Unpublished doctoral dissertation, Massachusetts Institute of Technology, 1970.

Snyder, R. A., Raben, C. S., and Farr, J. L. "A Model for the Systematic Evaluation of Human Resources Development Programs." *Academy of Management Review,* 1980, *5* (3), 431–444.

Solie, R. J. "Employment Effects of Retraining the Unemployed." *Industrial and Labor Relations Review,* 1968, *21,* 210–225.

Stromsdorfer, E. W. "Determinants of Economic Success in Retraining the Unemployed: The West Virginia Experience." *Journal of Human Resources Review,* 1968, *3,* 139–158.

Triandis, H. C., Feldman, J. M., Weldon, D. E., and Harvey, W. M. "Designing Preemployment Training for the Hard To Employ: A Cross-Cultural Psychological Approach." *Journal of Applied Psychology,* 1974, *59,* 687–693.

U.S. Office of Personnel Management. *A Guide to the Participant Action Plan Approach.* Washington, D.C.: U.S. Government Printing Office, 1980.

Watson, J. G., and Rowe, C. D. "Training of Operative Employees Contributing to a Successful Native American Enterprise: A Case Study." *Training and Development Journal,* 1976, *30,* 10–15.

Wirtz, W., and Goldstein, H. "Measurement and Analysis of Work Training." *Monthly Labor Review,* September, 1975, pp. 19–26.

Dan Baugher is an associate professor in the Lubin Schools of Business Administration of management, Pace University, New York City. He is interested in the prediction of socially relevant criteria, such as employee effectiveness, through an examination of individual differences. He has worked as a consultant on problems of measurement and prediction for AT&T and Hardee's Food Systems, Inc.

*Comprehensive assessment can lead to informed
decision making in our schools. In the past, the focus
of evaluation has been too narrow.*

Comprehensive Assessment
of Educational Systems

John B. Gormly

Anyone who looks at our investment in current educational systems easily
stands in awe of the undertaking. Billions of hours of adult labor and
billions of hours from the lives of children are involved. Billions of dollars
are spent each year. The extent of the resources committed illustrates the
importance that formal education holds for us. Why do we value public
education so highly; what do we expect or desire from this massive investment of resources? These are questions about the goals of educational
systems.

At the most general level, we intend that public education should
have two interdependent effects on children. First, public education should
provide formal training and acculturation so that the children can become
"good citizens" who can participate in a complex, technological society as
effective adults. Second, public education should provide children with a
broad set of experiences which enable them to realize their talents and
interests so that they may live richer, more enjoyable lives. These can be
considered the ultimate goals of public education.

In this chapter I will look at the goals of educational systems and
the effective and efficient fulfillment of those goals. The orientation
taken here, with its focus on institutional goals, is not the only view-
point from which one can evaluate the operations of organizations

D. Baugher (Ed.). *New Directions for Program Evaluation: Measuring Effectiveness*, no. 11.
San Francisco: Jossey-Bass, September 1981

(Connolly and Deutsch, 1980). I will return to the issue of goals later in this chapter.

To fulfill their purposes, educational systems must allow for decisions that give direction to school programs. Effective assessment can assist the persons making administrative decisions by bringing forth clear, objective information that is relevant to the decisions being made. When we think about the administration of educational systems, we must not only consider the principals and superintendents of schools, who are most likely to arrange for any assessment programs. We must also remember that classroom teachers carry out the moment-to-moment task of directing the educational activities of children and have the direct responsibility as well as the opportunity for fulfilling the goals of public education. Research has documented that teachers direct the activities of the classroom without much influence and supervision from other teachers, principals, or superintendents, although neither teachers nor administrators seem to be aware of this independence (Cohen, 1976; Meyer and others, 1978).

The Meaning of Comprehensive Assessment

I use the term "comprehensive assessment" to refer to a strategy of assessment design in which we (1) measure multiple indexes of performance in schools rather than a single area of performance such as academic attainment and (2) allow for a sequence of studies by which the problems, findings, and limitations of the previous study can be taken into consideration in setting the procedure for each successive study. Perhaps an example from my early research in education will set the stage for a consideration of the advantages of this strategy.

An Example of Comprehensive Assessment. Two investigations were conducted on male juvenile delinquents at a state training school (Gormly and Nittoli, 1971; 1974). As is often the case for juvenile offenders in institutions, these students were seriously deficient in basic academic skills, including language skills. Although the staff considered remedial education an important aspect of a correctional program, the students often resisted and avoided participation in the academic aspects of the school. Because the students were required by law to attend school, the avoidance and resistance took place in the classroom. The students were disruptive, physically aggressive, or not cooperative. Thus, even though the teachers and resources were available for remedial education, the results were that the teachers spent a good percentage of their time and effort maintaining order and discipline at the expense of teaching academic subjects.

We recognized that the students had already experienced years of failure in school settings and that the avoidance of more failure experiences could be a powerful motive in the behavior of these students. Our program was intended to bring about a rapid improvement in language skills. To effect this improvement, we had to deal with the avoidance of lessons. The particular procedure we used is more fully explained in the reported articles (Gormly and Nittoli, 1971; 1974) and is not the focus here, but, briefly, we attempted to remove the potential for failure and increase the opportunity for academic improvement by allowing each student to be his own evaluator and by preparing individualized lessons that matched each student's level of mastery and interests.

Since the obvious purpose of these programs was to accelerate academic achievement in reading skills, we tested several aspects of the student's achievement in reading (speed, accuracy, vocabulary, and comprehension) before and after his participation in the program. Over the duration of summer school, the average gain (if the two studies are considered together) in the various aspects of reading performance was equivalent to approximately two grade levels. In the second study, the students, who ranged in age from fourteen to nineteen and averaged at the fifth-grade level of achievement in reading skills, left the program reading at the seventh-grade level.

Although the programs appeared to be successful enough, what I have described is only their impact on academic tasks. Ongoing observations of the students revealed a variety of changes in areas outside of their performance on a test of reading skills. When we consider these additional changes we develop a more useful view of the complex interdependencies at work.

Additional Effects of the Reading Program. We observed that several students chose to have additional classroom lessons, which they could do in place of the time they were free for recreation. In the recreational period, they could swim, play softball, or participate in a variety of activities considered to be play. They received no acknowledgment or extrinsic reward for taking additional lessons rather than participating in recreational activities; it was strictly a personal preference. They lined up outside the classroom, and if there was space, they were admitted into the room.

Our records indicated that for the sixty-four students who participated in the programs (which involved approximately sixty class days) there was only one disciplinary incident. In their regular classrooms, disciplinary problems were often a daily event.

After-the-program interviews with the students made it clear that they were interested in being academically successful and that it is not true that students who do poorly in school and are disruptive do not yearn for academic accomplishment. These students had believed that they could not be successful in school, and they had set up defensive patterns of behavior that minimized the impact of their deficiencies. Disruptive, defensive behavior was a way for the students to inflate both their public images—what teachers and peers thought of them—and their self-images.

As a result of multiple measures of performance, the impact of the reading programs can be seen more fully. Attitudes limited and directed behavior in the classroom; by taking away the obstacles to academic achievement (fear of failure), we prepared the way for involvement in academic learning without external reward. With involvement in appropriate lessons came a rapid improvement in the skills of reading; with accomplishment in the classroom, students sometimes selected self-instruction in reading over recreational activities.

Our second study was built on what we learned from the first. The data show that the second program was more successful than the first. Had we had the opportunity for continuous revision and assessment, I am confident that a more complete and concrete picture of the impact of the program would have been developed. This is not a trivial concern. The program just described, which anyone would have to consider successful, was not continued in the school. While we had considered the implementation of the procedures and assessed the impact of the program on multiple areas of performance for the students, we did not attend to the impact of this "new" procedure on the teachers. As indicated earlier, teachers make the direct decisions about the activities in the classroom. Following the idea of comprehensive assessment, the next study on the reading program will include an evaluation of the impact of this program on the classroom teachers.

The Advantages of Comprehensive Assessment. Recent activities directed at evaluating educational programs have led to the "discovery" that activities in educational settings are many and complex. Researchers have long realized the many difficulties of research and evaluation in nonlaboratory, social settings. One direction to follow is to conduct research where it can be done neatly (for example, in a laboratory). An examination of the procedures used in studies reported in journals of social psychology, for example, will demonstrate that the great majority of these studies are not of the real world. Although they have eliminated many of the difficulties of studying human performance in the setting in which it occurs, the large issue of the relevance of these studies for understanding performance as it typically occurs is not considered. Of course, irrelevance of the research is an important concern.

Connolly and Deutsch (1980), Fincher (1978), and Schroder (1978) have published accounts of the difficulties of assessment research in real-life settings. It would be easy to let these actual or anticipated difficulties inhibit research. The strategy of comprehensive assessment attempts to deal with the complexity inherent in naturalistic, social situations by capturing the complexity with measures of several aspects of performance and by providing for successive revision and inquiry.

In the past, assessment of educational systems was something conducted at some particular point in the life of a program. Under those conditions, the focus of what was included in the assessment project was quite narrow. It was not really the school program that was being assessed, but a small part of it that someone considered to be representative of the whole or important in itself. This limited approach is no longer satisfactory, and strategies of assessment have to progress.

We might hope that the specialist in assessment would come to the school with a ready-to-go technology that would reveal in one study the workings, the effectiveness, and the efficiency of the educational program. Such definitiveness is not possible. Parents, teachers, and researchers alike know that every answer to a question leads to another question, and that usually the answer leads to several new questions. Although this process may be bothersome, frustrating to our desire for certainty in an answer, this process leads to knowledge. Knowledge comes through the refinement of information—refinement that is possible when there are a series of related questions and answers. Strategies of comprehensive assessment will yield information that is most representative of the complex interdependencies in the school setting. Comprehensive assessment thus leads to informed decisions about the operation of the school.

The Question of Goals

However useful ultimate goals are for gaining resources for education and for giving educational activities broad direction, they do not lead the assessment specialist to specific, measurable events. Goals such as "the development of good citizens" refer to some time in the far future for most school children, and, if for no other reason than that, cannot be the basis for assessment. The concrete goals of public education, stated in a way that could lead to measurement of those goals, remain unspecified.

We might interview teachers, principals, and superintendents and ask them to explain the specific goals and methods designed to realize those ultimate goals in their schools. Meyer and others (1978) made such an inquiry part of their study of the degree to which schools and districts are coordinated organizations. They reported that rather than consensus about the policies and practices within schools and within districts, there primarily are differences among teachers, principals, and superintendents. Furthermore, these differences are not recognized by the educators. This research and similar research (Cohen, 1976) support the position that educational systems are not coordinated systems wherein teachers implement the policies or philosophies of the administration. The principal knows about such budget-related activities of the classroom as the kind of reading material there or the number of paid aids. The principal, in general, does not know about the activities of the teacher, the content of lessons, or the style of discipline. To understand the goals of educational activities, we might best focus on the teachers.

Returning for a moment to the strategy of interviewing the teachers to determine the goals or purposes underlying the activities in the classroom, we must recognize that as we go about living our lives and interacting with others, we generally are not aware of the specific intentions, purposes, or goals that direct our interactions. The teachers' responses to the questions about goals are very likely to be different from the goals of the moment-to-moment activities of the classroom. Let us begin to answer the question about goals by saying that no one can state with any degree of certainty what is occurring in classrooms. Because of that level of ignorance, it is unlikely that anyone can tell us about the purposes of educational activities.

Assessing the Actual Goals. The following section will describe an attempt to uncover the goals or purposes that underlie the direction that the teacher gives to the activities in the classroom. I am assuming that human behavior is purposeful or directed toward bringing about particular outcomes or experiences; that is, it is goal-directed rather than random.

First I will describe the procedure and then consider some of the limitations. This procedure is similar to one I use in building a personality theory of an individual. In that work, I am interested in finding the aims or goals operating in a person's life and the specific ways that person attempts to fulfill those aims. From that research I have found that when considering some recent event in his or her life, a person can very often state his or her intentions regarding participation in the event. Awareness of intention, of course, does not ensure that those intentions are always or often fulfilled.

The events of the classroom can be sampled by brief two- to five-minute videotapings at random intervals throughout the school day. The teacher videotaped should view the tape at a time that is convenient yet as close as possible to the time of taping. Teachers are simply asked to describe the purpose or purposes of their activities during the interval taped.

The next part of this project is to formulate a finite list of categories of purposes or goals that encompass the responses given by the teachers. The extensive literature on categories of human motives can be used to assist the development of the list of goals underlying the moment-to-moment activities of the teachers (Murray, 1938).

Examples of the Categories. Although the list constructed by the assessment personnel would depend on the actual responses given by the teachers, the categories might include the following: to inform or to explain academic material; to control unacceptable behavior; to enhance status, position, or image; to reprimand, ridicule, or punish; to attract attention; to entertain; to give sympathy and support; and so on.

After they develop a tentative list of motives, the assessment personnel are in a position to go back to the original format of systematically sampling the activities of the teacher. Now when reviewing the tape, the teacher simply indicates the items on the list of motives that best describe his or her motivation. If no items fit the motive, then that information is useful for successive revisions of the list.

Having used the procedures described above, we arrive at a description of the proportion of interactions that were directed toward achieving particular purposes as well as a description of the specific activities which occurred. For example, we can estimate the percentage of the teacher's activities that were directed at academic attainment and the form those activities took.

Directing the Activities of the Classroom. As stated earlier, assessment can assist the person making administrative decisions by bringing forth clear, objective information that is relevant to the decisions being made. The procedure described above is directly relevant to the teachers and the decisions they make in their moment-to-moment activities in the classroom. Of course, this method is useful only insofar as the teacher is willing to participate. The teachers need to see that the purpose of the project is to assist them—that the assessment specialist is to the teacher what the lawyer is to the businessman, a resource. Administrators should view this project not as supervision of the teachers but as a tool for effective education. Vital to success is the administrator's recognition of the independent position of the teacher.

The Preferred Goals

What intermediate goals would we prefer to have underlying the educational activity? We cannot have optimal decisions about effective and efficient methods of education without a clear set of goals that the methods are to achieve.

As a beginning, there are at least three facets to the process of acculturating children. These facets are included among the responsibilities of the public schools: academic attainment, the development of personal and social behaviors that permit behavioral adaptation to the culture, and the transmission of attitudes and values that are compatible with those of the society. The first questions are these: What, specifically, is the meaning of each of these concepts? What are the relevant and observable indicators of each of these goals?

It is no easy task, but it is important that we translate terms like "personal and social behaviors that permit behavioral adaptation to the culture" into acts that are clearly observable in the performance of school children. The task is made larger because the concrete references for these goals will vary according to the ages of the children and may vary from one region of the country to another. Further, cultures are not static. They change, and in the age of space travel, biological revolutions, computers, and nuclear power, the culture is changing rapidly. The task of the schools to participate in the acculturation of the children is made more difficult by the shifting requirements and meanings of "behavioral adaptation to the culture." In light of these considerations, school systems would benefit by establishing procedures for defining their goals in concrete terms and then making those procedures ongoing so that the concrete referents would be periodically revised.

While we might begin to refine the meaning of the three goals by proceeding rationally, only a detailed understanding of the lives of children and how the goals are already present there will lead to a specific account of the performance the schools are aiming to develop.

Academic Considerations. Teaching academic skills is the most obvious mission of the school. One primary concern is to have children become proficient in language skills. There are many subareas of language skills: presenting ideas in speaking, presenting ideas in writing, understanding others through attentive listening, understanding others through fast and accurate reading. Within these subareas there are even more molecular skills such as grammar, vocabulary, and style. Calling this complex collection of skills language, can lead, unfortunately, to their being viewed as equivalent to one another. In fact, a single student can vary widely in the mastery of the various components. For example, a student may be good in reading, average in grammar, and poor in style of presentation in speaking but not in writing. We need tests that describe more precisely the student's level of attainment within any area of study, whether it be language, mathematics, humanities, or sciences. This information, in turn, would be most helpful if we had programs that were individualized so that they matched the student's levels of performance within any subject area. Just as two persons can score 100 on an IQ test and have widely different scores on the items and subscales that make up the test, students who score at the same grade level on standardized tests of language skills may have quite different underlying accomplishments and need quite different educational programs.

Educators have not sufficiently considered the implications of individual differences in achievements, abilities, interests, and rates of learning. One implication is straightforward: education is at its best when individualized. Sometimes we find that there are two or three levels of instruction for any particular grade; the question of homogeneous versus heterogeneous groupings of students on the basis of current performance levels is overly debated. The question is a misleading one because the real issue is whether there should be groupings at all. Under ideal conditions there would be a specific educational program for each student. My belief is that with such tailor-made programs we would see very rapid mastery of traditional academic subject matter.

The development of individualized programs of instruction hinges on the concept of an established system of assessment of the various molecular aspects of academic material. The function of this system is to identify the student's mastery of the many components of language, arithmetic and so on. Along with this assessment system, we need a complement of individualized lessons. When we consider the development these two systems would require, we know we are not going to achieve these tools overnight. We can, however, move in the direction of individualized education by using programs that have already been developed (see Gormly and Nittoli, 1974); with the tremendous resources that have been committed to educational programs, we could easily develop them further. This would be a likely outcome if assessment were an ongoing part of the school system.

There are certainly other factors that interfere with academic attainment, and I would like to acknowledge them here. At the request of the director of education of a training school, I conducted a detailed assessment of forty-one students who were nonreaders or who were reading at a minimal level. Only ten students had serious perceptual or intellectual deficiencies. The great majority had uncorrected hearing or visual disabilities and emotional or personality problems. The point is that there are a variety of problems interfering with education that do not involve instruction per se.

Personal and Social Skills. There has been too little consideration of the role schools play in teaching personal and social skills and too little information about how teachers explicitly and implicitly influence social and personal behavior. Bronfenbrenner (1979) describes schools as an alienating setting, cooperating with the trend that isolates children from the broader society.

Report cards traditionally have acknowledged social and personal skills. Students receive marks for such skills as "conduct," "effort," and "ability to get along with others." These marks are an explicit recognition of the involvement of the school in these areas. Unfortunately, lesson plans reflect neither content nor methods for teaching these skills.

What shall we consider good behavioral adaptation to be? When I taught large lecture courses in child psychology, one of the requirements for the course was that students observe a local kindergarten class to see what, in their judgments, were problems in the behavior of the children there. Several hundred college students participated in this project. They were to describe the specific incident they considered a problem and to name the general category of behavior under which the incident fit. The behavioral problem most often observed was social withdrawal from peers. The reports described a large number of children who oriented themselves toward the adult in charge and actively avoided interactions with other children. The second most observed problem was physical aggression.

The method used by the college students could be modified and improved upon by assessment personnel. Again, by videotaping numerous samplings of the behavior of children of many ages in a variety of settings, the person conducting the assessment would acquire an objective record.

These records could then be reviewed by a group of raters for two kinds of incidents. The raters could identify incidents during which a particular child was engaged in behavior considered desirable by the raters. In other words, the raters are told to "catch the child being good." When there is high agreement among raters that certain behaviors benefit both the performer and the group, the raters in essence identify a specific and concrete goal for the kind of personal or social behavior to encourage in a child of that age. There is also a record of how frequently acts of that general category occur in any particular setting. The videotape serves as a specific record of personal or social adaptation from which to build lesson plans. In this way social and personal goals are included in the deliberate education of the child.

A similar process can be applied to student behavior that interferes with the well being of the group or the person performing the act or to behavior that disrupts academic lessons. Again, there should be high agreement that certain acts are undesirable. Similarly, there would be an objective record of undesirable behavior for each age group of students in schools. This behavior could be discussed during the training of teachers. Negative behaviors could be anticipated as a normal occurrence in the classroom, and lesson plans could be planned to minimize its effect in the classroom or its occurrence.

This process is not an attempt to make all children the same or to bring about rigorous behavioral control in the classroom. It is a deliberate attempt to encourage those kinds of behaviors that promote the well being of a child in a way that is appropriate for the age of the child. Teachers are quite attentive to disruptive or "crazy" behavior in children. As a result, efforts to establish harmony and order are frequently restrictive or punitive. Punishment by the teacher in turn sets up a relationship of noncooperation between the teacher and some children. When the teacher can work from the positive position of knowing what is beneficial to the child and the class and what is reasonable for a child of that age, the teaching of those styles of behaving will naturally result in a reduction of undesirable behavior and improve the relationship between the teacher and the children.

The particular categories of behavior involved and the specific form those behaviors take at a given age await a formal assessment project. Below are listed a few general categories from my own work.

From the area of social adjustment, we could teach and encourage behavior on the positive side of the continuum:

1. Co-operative   versus   Antagonistic, aggressive, and exploitative
2. Sociable, friendly,   versus   Social avoidance or withdrawal; critical;
   relaxed with others;   rejecting others
   accepting

3. Considerate of the   versus   Fulfills own desires at the expense of others
   rights of others,   or without regard for effect on others.
   helpful

From the area of personal adjustment, we could teach and encourage behavior on the positive side of the continuum:

---

1. Instrumental com-   Incompetent in achieving personal goals;
   petence in achiev-   versus   the child lets or gets others to do it for him
   ing personal goals;   or her
   the child does it
   himself or herself

2. Anticipates suc-   Anticipates or fears failure, easily dis-
   cess and perseveres versus   couraged; quits in the face of difficulty
   in the face of
   difficulties

3. Relaxed in a   versus   Anxious
   variety of settings

4. Sense of humor,   versus   Solemn, moody, grouchy
   playful

5. Curious   versus   Bored

Attitudes and Values. A third goal of education is the transmission of attitudes and values that promote individual development and are compatible with those of the broader society. Here, again, there is very little in the education of our teachers or in the structure of the school's curriculum that specifies the attitudes we want to develop or correct or describes the methods for doing so. Yet even young children have attitudes and values; they have them with respect to themselves—ideas of their own worth and place in the family, school, and society—and they have attitudes and values about other people. The importance of the child's evaluative view of self, of others, and the events of living cannot be overrated. These views are taken to be true by the person who holds them; for the most part these views are not susceptible to being examined or corrected. They are private events, and they are used to give meaning to experiences rather than to be corrected by experiences. We would like the child to have attitudes and values that promote the well being of the child and the society.

What do children believe about themselves and others, and how does this belief system change as children become older? There are several well-developed methods for building inventories of attitudes and values (see Fishbein, 1967, for example). The assessment specialist could easily build an inventory for children of a given age. From such measures we would know specifically and concretely about childrens' evaluative views. Again, using high agreement among raters from the school and community, we could identify a set of beliefs that we would want to promote. These would be values and attitudes that we believe enhance the child and society. We could also identify a set of beliefs that we would want to correct because they are seriously incorrect or because they do not promote the well being of the child or society. With this specific information about goals, we would then be in the position to design a program for teaching attitudes and values. This is not an attempt to take over a child's mind and create uniformity. (That is not possible with any technology that I know of.) What I am describing are specific, age-appropriate goals that we learn from studying the children themselves. In my own work, I suggest these as profitable areas: self-esteem (children would learn to accept and like themselves and to feel a worthiness in themselves); confidence (children would recognize their abilities to do many things to their own satisfaction); tolerance (children would recognize that people are of different abilities, temperaments, races, and cultures and that this diversity is a natural and beneficial quality to the human race).

Summary: Students and Educational Systems

The ultimate goals of educational systems and the preferred (or intermediate) goals (academic attainment, development of personal and social skills, and transmission of attitudes and values) provide broad direction to educational activities, but the specific, immediate goals of the day-to-day activities of education have never been specified or determined. Given that there is no detailed information about the specific activities of children and teachers in the classroom, we are not yet in a position to specify realistic immediate goals. A starting step is to observe (videotape), describe, and classify the actual activities of students and teachers. From that base we would be better able to consider whether a particular event promotes, inhibits, or is irrelevant to the goals of public education. We are a long way from consensus about the goals of educational systems. At this point, we would do better to study the actual goals of the teachers than to evaluate how effective a program is in meeting some poorly conceptualized, ideal goal.

Still, there is a long history of criticism about the activities and effects of schooling on children. We hear from Piaget (1962) that the procedures of traditional education hamper the development of reasoning. Bikson (1978) writes that the format of traditional education inhibits curiosity, creativity, and active participation in learning while the teachers are rewarding conformity and passivity. Certainly, we need to assess the activities and effects of schooling with respect to these complaints.

We need schools that not only educate children but also attract them—schools that children would choose to attend even if we did not compel them to with laws and threats of a dismal future for the undereducated. When we consider the resources adults give to education and the natural, intrinsic motive of children to learn and become competent (White, 1960), it is not so outrageous to expect that children should freely elect schooling.

For many children, school is a place they want to leave; recess and lunch are their favorite periods. We need to refine the operation of schools so that they are a place where children choose to go; comprehensive assessment is a strategy that can assist educators in improving the nature of formal education. We should not wait too long; suppose we opened the schools one morning, and the children refused to enter?

References

Bikson, T. K. "The Status of Children's Intellectual Rights." *Journal of Social Issues*, 1978, *34* (2), 69–86.

Bronfenbrenner, U. "Contexts of Child Rearing: Problems and Prospects." *American Psychologist*, 1979, *34* (10), 844–850.

Cohen, E. G. "Organization and Instruction in Elementary Schools." Technical Report No. 50. Stanford, Calif.: Center for Research and Development in Teaching, Stanford University, 1976.

Connolly, T., and Deutsch, S. J. "Performance Measurement: Some Conceptual Issues." *Evaluation and Program Planning*, 1980, *3* (1), 35–43.

Fincher, C. "Program Monitoring in Higher Education." In D. Grant (Ed.), *New Directions for Program Evaluation: Monitoring Ongoing Programs*, no. 3. San Francisco: Jossey-Bass, 1978.

Fishbein, M. *Readings in Attitude Theory and Measurement.* New York: Wiley, 1967.

Gormly, J., and Nittoli, M. J. "Rapid Improvement of Reading Skills in Juvenile Delinquents." *Journal of Experimental Education*, 1971, *40* (2), 45–48.

Gormly, J., and Nittoli, M. J. "A Psychological Approach to Reading." *Journal of Correctional Education*, 1974, *4* (1), 21–25.

Meyer, J. W., Scott, R. W., Cole, S., and Intili, J. K. "Instructional Dissensus and Institutional Consensus in Schools." In M. W. Meyer and Associates (Eds.), *Environments and Organizations*, San Francisco: Jossey-Bass, 1978.

Murray, H. A. *Explorations in Personality.* New York: Oxford University Press, 1938.

Piaget, J. *The Child's Concept of Number.* London: Routledge & Kegan Paul, 1962.

Schroder, H. M. "Organizational Control: Monitoring Ongoing Programs." In S. B. Anderson and C. D. Coles (Eds.), *New Directions for Program Evaluation: Exploring Purposes and Dimensions*, no. 1. San Francisco: Jossey-Bass, 1978.

White, R. W. "Competence and the Psychosexual Stages of Development." In M. R. Jones (Ed.), *Nebraska Symposium of Motivation.* Lincoln: University of Nebraska Press, 1960.

John B. Gormly is an associate professor of psychology, Rutgers University. He has served for several years as a consultant to educational programs in various schools and agencies.

Regression techniques can be used to study the progress of exceptional schools—those whose children perform much better or worse than could have been predicted from past achievement.

Identifying Exceptional Schools

Gary Kippel

The considerable responsibility invested in schools to educate our children makes it especially crucial that techniques be developed to identify and monitor school progress. In particular, the identification of schools manifesting exceptional progress is essential so that successful educational practices can be examined and replicated elsewhere. Similarly, schools manifesting relatively low student achievement must be identified because such schools are most in need of change and support. The purpose of this chapter, therefore, is to illustrate techniques which might be used, in conjunction with other measures, to identify exceptional schools.

In this chapter, exceptional school progress is defined in terms of a relationship between student output and input. This approach differs from most reports of standardized test results in that most reports fail to provide a measure of progress from one year to the next. The general approach followed in this chapter, as described in the following sections, has been to

This chapter is based upon a longitudinal study conducted jointly by the Board of Education of the City of New York and the Educational Testing Service, Princeton, New Jersey, from 1975 through 1978. The Board of Education component was headed by Charles I. Schonhaut, Senior Assistant to the Chancellor. The Educational Testing Service component was headed by Garlie A. Forehand, Director of Educational Research.

D. Baugher (Ed.). *New Directions for Program Evaluation: Measuring Effectiveness*, no. 11. San Francisco: Jossey-Bass, September 1981 express school progress in terms of an expected or predicted output. School progress, in this sense, is considered exceptional when the ratio between its actual output and its expected output exceeds a criterion established for this purpose. In other words, this chapter discusses a way of identifying schools that have made more or less progress than expected.

To illustrate the use of regression techniques to identify exceptional schools, indices for grades three, four, and five in approximately 600 New York City elementary schools were generated. Schools with exceptionally positive or negative indices were then identified. Finally, characteristics of these schools with exceptional indices were examined briefly.

It is noted that the illustrative calculations in this chapter were based on raw scores. The same statistical techniques could be employed with grade-equivalent or other transformed scores. However, the use of raw scores in these calcuations is most desirable. Unfortunately, some school systems report test results as grade-equivalent scores. Such grade-equivalent measures are technically deficient and, consequently, are subject to statistical distortion and misinterpretation (see Baugher's chapter on remedial training; and Cronbach, 1970, p. 98; United States Department of Health, Education and Welfare, 1975, pp. 9–10).

Measuring School Progress with Regression Techniques

Regression analyses (see Draper and Smith, 1966; Kerlinger and Pedhazur, 1973) are statistical techniques useful in identifying schools that have progressed more or less than would be predicted on the basis of their past performance. One earlier set of test scores is used as a predictor and a later set of scores is used as a criterion variable. In this chapter, for example, the regression analysis for each grade employs both 1977 and 1978 test scores.

Regression analyses result in regression equations that specify linear or curvilinear relationships that can be depicted graphically. For example, Figure 1 illustrates the relationship between actual later scores and scores predicted on the basis of earlier scores. In this manner, a forty-five–degree regression line would represent a progress ratio (that is, a ratio of earlier test scores to later test scores) of 1.00. Furthermore, schools obtaining scores above the regression line have actual later scores that exceed their expected achievement. Similarly, schools obtaining scores below the regression line have actual later scores that fall below their expected achievement. This conceptual framework was also employed by Astin (1962) to assess productivity of undergraduate institutions. See Astin (1968) for further elaboration.

In Figure 1, each of the dots surrounding the regression line represents one school. The distance between the point or dot representing each school and the regression line is called a residual and is an index or measure

Figure 1. Illustrative Regression Line for Sixty-Two Schools

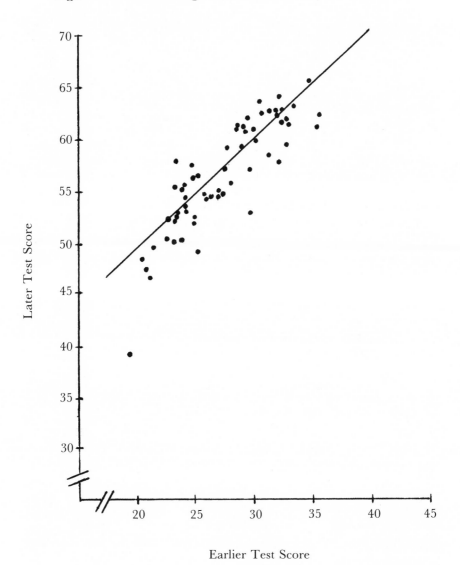

of school progress. In effect, the residual is the difference between the actual later mean test score and that score predicted on the basis of each school's previous mean test score. In other words, the residual can be thought of as a measure of how much an obtained score is higher or lower than predicted. In Figure 1, for example, a school represented by a dot above the regression line has a positive residual and can be thought of as having made greater progress than predicted on the basis of its previous test performance. In similar manner, a school represented by a point below the regression line has a negative residual and can be thought of as having made somewhat less progress than predicted. It is noted that similar analyses, focusing on individual students rather than schools, could be used to describe individual student progress.

A more complex model would involve the calculation of more than one regression equation to represent different schools. For example, one regression equation might represent progress of schools in relatively high socioeconomic neighborhoods, while a second equation might represent schools in relatively low socioeconomic neighborhoods. Such models, however, may imply one set of expectations for schools in wealthier communities and different expectations for other schools in poorer communities. Such double standards are not desirable.

In contrast with more traditional reports of test results, regression analyses (1) result in a longitudinal measure of school progress in that two separate school means, obtained respectively at an earlier and later time, are required for each school; (2) provide a relative measure, in that each school's progress is compared to the progress of all schools included in the regression equation; and (3) yield standard errors of estimate that aid in the interpretation of individual school indices and also provide a basis to define exceptional school progress operationally.

Identifying Exceptional Schools

One regression equation was calculated for each of grades three, four, and five. Each of these analyses employed both 1977 and 1978 data. Specifically, reading comprehension raw scores were obtained from the Comprehensive Test of Basic Skills (Form S) administered in 1977 and the California Achievement Test (Form D) administered in 1978. For each year, data were obtained for grades three (52,539 students), four (51,915 students), and five (53,159 students) from 616, 616, and 612 elementary schools, respectively. In all grades, the time span between test administrations was one year.

Calculating the Regression Equations. The regression equations were calculated with individual student test scores. These test scores were employed in the calculation of regression equations because some people expressed the view that such equations, in contrast to equations calculated with scores aggregated by schools, were easier to understand as reflective of student growth and, as such, were more acceptable. There is evidence, however, that regression equations based upon all students mask distinctions within and between groups (see Burstein and Miller, 1978). Future analyses, therefore, must carefully examine the desirability of using regression equations based upon either individual student test scores or scores aggregated by school. (See Convey, 1975; Dyer and others, 1969; Dyer, 1971; Marco, 1974; and McDonald and others, 1972 for discussions of other regression models.)

Two consecutive reading comprehension test scores were obtained for each student (see McDonald and others, 1972, p. 56). For each of the three grades, subsequently, the regression of individual student 1978 scores on individual student 1977 scores was calculated. Data were examined to determine the appropriateness of the linear model. Trends beyond the linear were neither significant nor meaningful. In addition, examination of the data points and regression lines and the relatively high squared correlations provided evidence for the appropriateness of the linear regression model.

Regression coefficients and intercepts comprise the regression equations for each grade. For example, the regression coefficient and intercept for grade five were .643 and 2.238, respectively. Consequently, the regression equation for grade five was: $Y_5' = .643X_5 + 2.238$, where Y_5' is the predicted 1978 grade five mean test score and X_5 is the actual 1977 grade five mean test score. Similarly, the regression equations for grades four and three were: $Y_4' = .602X_4 + 4.652$ and $Y_3' = .410X_3 + 6.826$, respectively. Regression equations are used, with the 1977 predictor scores, to calculate predicted 1978 criterion scores and also to draw regression lines. When used to draw regression lines, the regression coefficient is the slope of the regression line and the intercept is the point at which the regression line intercepts the vertical axis.

Obtaining Indices for Each School. Next, the individual student test scores were aggregated to obtain 1977 and 1978 mean test scores for grades three, four, and five in each school. Each 1977 mean score was then entered into the previously calculated regression equation for each of the three grades, respectively. This procedure resulted in predicted 1978 mean scores for each grade in each school. Subsequently, these predicted 1978 mean scores were subtracted from each of the respective actual 1978 mean scores to obtain a residual or measure of the difference between what was predicted and what was achieved. For example, if the 1977 mean test score for grade five (that is, X_5) for a specific school was 32.29, the predicted 1978 grade five mean score for that school would be: $Y_5' = .643(32.29) + 2.238 = 23.00$. Next, the actual 1978 grade five mean score would be obtained. In this hypothetical example, it might be 25.25. Therefore, the predicted 1978 score (23.00) would be subtracted from the actual 1978 score (25.25) to obtain a residual for grade five in this school of + 2.25. In summary, by using the regression equation based upon individual student scores and the mean scores aggregated by school for each grade, residual scores were calculated for grades three, four and five in each elementary school.

Identifying Schools with Exceptional Indices. The main objective of the study was to identify schools that had made exceptional progress. Therefore, three things were done. First, only indices that were at least plus or minus one standard deviation from the mean were identified for each grade. This was accomplished by calculating the mean and standard deviation of the residuals for each grade. (In this chapter, exceptional indices were operationally defined by the criterion established for this purpose. Other criteria may be used. For a discussion of methods of determining school effectiveness following a regression analysis, see Convey, 1977. For a discussion of extreme residuals, which differ from exceptional residuals as discussed here, see Barnett and Lewis, 1978.) In our example, the means and standard deviations were .182 and 1.360, .193 and 2.027, and .154 and 1.946 for grades three, four, and five, respectively. This information was used to obtain cut-off points that were plus or minus one standard deviation from each mean. For example, in grade three the criteria were − 1.178 (that is, .182 − 1.360) for negative residuals and 1.542 (that is, .182 + 1.360) for positive residuals. Similarly, the criteria for negative and positive residuals were − 1.834 and 2.220, and − 1.792 and 2.100, for grades four and five, respectively. Only residuals above or below one standard deviation were considered in subsequent analyses. In effect, any residual within one standard deviation of the mean was excluded from further consideration.

Second, specific grades in some schools were eliminated if their mean scores were based upon relatively small numbers of students. In general, the fewer the test scores, the less confidence one may have in the stability of regression coefficients. Therefore, the means and standard deviations for the number of students tested in every grade were calculated. Then a cut-off point was established by identifying the number of students that was one standard deviation below the mean for each grade. These cut-off points were 23, 22, and 26 for grades three, four, and five, respectively. Consequently, any grade with the number of test scores below its respective criterion was eliminated from further consideration.

Third, only schools with exceptional indices in at least two of the three grades were retained. It seemed that schools with consistent (that is, all positive or all negative) exceptional indices in at least two grades would more likely reflect exceptional overall school progress than schools with only one exceptional grade. In other words, the more grades with exceptional indices, the more likely that the entire school had made exceptional progress.

In our example, it was found that thirty schools had exceptionally positive indices in at least two grades and thirty-seven schools had exceptionally negative indices in at least two grades. Six schools had positive indices in all three grades and four schools had negative indices in all three grades.

Mean Test Scores of Schools with Exceptional Indices

The number of schools with exceptional indices in each grade and the mean and standard deviation of the residuals for schools with both exceptionally positive and negative indices are presented in Table 1. In addition, the mean and standard deviations of the 1978 reading comprehension raw scores are presented.

Inasmuch as schools were selected as exceptional only if they obtained exceptional indices in more than one grade, the numbers in the column entitled "Number of Schools" in Table 1 include the same school more than one time. As a result, 66 separate grades three, four, and five within the 30 schools with exceptionally positive indices were examined. Similarly, 78 separate grades three, four, and five within the 37 schools with exceptionally negative indices were examined.

For schools with exceptionally positive residuals, the mean raw scores ranged from 22.68 in grade three to 28.73 in grade five. For schools with exceptionally negative residuals, the mean raw scores ranged from 15.51 in grade three to 17.40 in grade five.

Table 1. Descriptive Statistics

SCHOOLS WITH POSITIVE RESIDUALS:

Grade	Number of Schools (N = 30)	Residuals Mean	Residuals Standard Deviation	1978 Test Scores Mean	1978 Test Scores Standard Deviation
Three	25	1.90	.35	22.68	1.12
Four	21	2.94	.66	25.86	2.47
Five	20	3.09	.93	28.73	2.27

SCHOOLS WITH NEGATIVE RESIDUALS:

Grade	Number of Schools (N = 37)	Residuals Mean	Residuals Standard Deviation	1978 Test Scores Mean	1978 Test Scores Standard Deviation
Three	32	− 1.82	.48	15.51	1.49
Four	22	− 2.52	.42	15.86	1.81
Five	24	− 2.70	.68	17.40	1.90

The relationship between residuals and the number of students was examined to determine if residuals are related to the number of students in each grade. A total of six correlations between both positive and negative residuals and the number of students contributing data in grades three, four, and five were calculated. Only the correlation for grade five negative residuals and number of students was found to be significantly greater than zero (r = .46; p <.05). In the other five instances, no significant relationship was found between the residuals and the number of students.

Characteristics of Schools with Exceptional Indices

The following section demonstrates how relationships between residuals and school characteristics were examined. In addition, there is an assessment of how schools with positive or negative residuals differ from each other. It should be noted that the following represents only preliminary analyses and is meant to be illustrative rather than conclusive.

There have been many studies concerned with the impact of school resources on achievement. A large proportion of these investigations have been based upon or stimulated by *Equality of Educational Opportunity* by Coleman and others (1966). These include, for example, Jencks and others (1972), Mayeske and others (1972), and Mosteller and Moynihan (1972). Additional studies of student achievement and school characteristics include Brookover and Lezotte (1977); Bryant and others (1974); Edmonds and Frederiksen (1978); Klepak (1974); Rutter and others (1979); Sewell and others (1976); Summers and Wolfe (1975); and University of the State of New York (1972, 1973, 1976). The main consequence of these works appears to be a lack of consensus regarding both findings and analytic methods (see Armor, 1972; Burstein, 1977; Burstein and Miller, 1978; Hanushek and Kain, 1972; Pedhazur, 1975; and Smith, 1972).

Averch and others (1972) and Spady (1973) surveyed studies of the impact on achievement of school resources and characteristics. Though valuable suggestions for future research are provided, there is a lack of definitive and conclusive findings. Averch and others (1972, p. 154) have stated the problem succinctly: "Research has not identified a variant of the existing system that is consistently related to students' educational outcomes."

The School Characteristics. Data were obtained for eight school characteristics representing three categories of variables. It is noted that some of these eight school characteristics are conventionally under school system control and are relatively easy to change, if it appears that change will positively influence student achievement. Further definition of the manner in which these measures of school characteristics were obtained can be found in *School Profiles 1976-1977* (pp. 5-18).

The first measure is a school building variable. Specifically, *percent utilization* is a measure of the usage of the school building in relation to its capacity. Capacity is defined as the ideal number of pupils that a school, given its educational program, can physically accommodate.

The next three variables refer to staff characteristics. First, *staff cost per pupil* is the total annual cost of pedagogical positions divided by the average daily register. Second, *pupil-teacher ratio* is the total number of teacher positions divided into the average daily register. Third, *percent experienced teachers* is the percent of teachers with five or more years of teaching experience.

The remaining four variables refer to student characteristics. *Average daily register* is the sum of the daily registers during the school year divided by the number of days in the school year. *Attendance* is the mean pupil attendance obtained by dividing the average daily register into the average daily attendance for ten attendance periods during the school year. *Student admissions* is the number of students admitted to a school divided by the average daily register for that year. Similarly, *student departures* is the number of students leaving a school divided by the average daily register for that year.

It is important to note that all eight characteristics are aggregated by school. This means that all data for each of these variables are reported as one overall mean score for the entire school. Therefore, it was not possible to obtain separate measures for each grade. All subsequent statistical analyses employ the overall school means for each of the eight variables.

Comparison Between Schools with Exceptionally Positive or Negative Indices. In order to compare schools with exceptionally positive or negative residuals, the mean and standard deviation of each school characteristic were calculated separately for the positive and negative groups (see Table 2); *t*-tests were then performed on the differences between means of the school characteristics to ascertain if these differences were significant in the statistical sense.

The procedure for computing *t* values (see Nie and others, 1975, pp. 268–271) included tests of homogeneity of variance. In addition, all *t*-tests were the two-tailed type because they assume no prior hypotheses about the direction of the difference between means.

The *t*-tests demonstrated statistically significant differences between schools with exceptionally positive and negative indices in at least one grade for six of the eight school characteristics examined. The statistically significant ratios obtained for Pupil Teacher Ratio and Student Attendance (and in grade five for Percent Utilization) indicate that the means of schools with positive indices were significantly higher than those for schools with negative indices. As indicated by the minus signs, the statistically significant ratios obtained for staff cost per pupil, average daily register, and student departures imply that the means of schools with

Table 2. Characteristics of Schools with Positive and Negative Residuals

School Characteristics	Grade	Schools With Positive Residuals (N = 30)			Schools With Negative Residuals (N = 37)			t-Test
		N	Mean	Standard Deviation	N	Mean	Standard Deviation	
Percent Utilization	Three	20	80.06	23.32	30	72.73	24.51	1.06
	Four	17	79.46	22.93	22	73.86	27.33	0.68
	Five	16	80.21	20.73	22	61.93	13.38	3.30[a]
Staff Cost per Pupil	Three	25	880.80	97.94	32	1,106.38	141.99	−6.78[b]
	Four	21	871.00	101.78	22	1,120.14	156.65	−6.15[b]
	Five	20	886.55	91.59	24	1,154.25	130.42	−7.72[b]
Pupil Teacher Ratio	Three	25	27.16	3.31	32	23.05	2.69	5.17[b]
	Four	21	27.58	3.35	22	22.84	3.07	4.84[b]
	Five	20	26.79	2.97	24	22.19	2.59	5.50[b]
Percent Experienced Teachers	Three	25	88.97	9.96	32	83.74	12.00	1.76
	Four	21	89.88	10.61	22	85.24	8.06	1.62
	Five	20	89.30	8.56	24	83.35	12.80	1.78
Average Daily Register	Three	25	629.80	260.93	32	839.50	285.72	−2.85[b]
	Four	21	620.90	224.27	22	842.36	237.90	−3.14[b]
	Five	20	628.95	244.23	24	756.63	270.14	−1.63
Student Attendance	Three	25	90.50	2.20	32	84.52	2.93	8.50[b]
	Four	21	90.83	2.44	22	85.21	2.31	7.76[b]
	Five	20	90.73	2.28	24	84.57	2.82	7.85[b]
Student Admissions	Three	25	35.19	10.51	31	40.71	9.97	−2.01
	Four	21	37.71	19.25	22	40.41	10.17	−0.57
	Five	20	39.85	18.32	23	38.523	8.51	−0.30
Student Departures	Three	25	19.37	8.46	32	34.62	10.52	−5.90[b]
	Four	21	19.08	7.43	22	32.17	6.89	−5.99[b]
	Five	20	18.99	8.69	24	34.16	11.86	−4.75[b]

[a] p < .05
[b] p < .01

negative indices were significantly higher than those for schools with positive indices.

The Relationship Between School Indices and School Characteristics

The following discussion bears upon the relationship between the school indices and the eight illustrative school characteristics. First, simple correlations between the residuals and school characteristics are discussed. Second, one example of multiple regression analysis is calculated.

It is important to note that the correlations reported here were based upon relatively small, homogeneous groups of schools. Specifically, correlations were calculated only for schools with exceptionally positive and negative residuals. In effect, the middle range of schools (that is, with residuals within one standard deviation from the mean) was excluded from these analyses. Each of these correlations, therefore, was based upon a relatively small number of schools, which is likely to be a more homogeneous sample when compared with all schools. As such, these correlations were based upon a truncated sample and are likely to be lower than one would expect if they were based upon a larger, more heterogeneous group of schools.

It should be noted, also, that examination of the relationships between school indices and school characteristics, as illustrated in this chapter, does not allow one to make causal inferences. Correlations significantly greater or less than zero indicate that some residuals and some school characteristics tend to covary. Although some correlations may be a result of one variable causing the other, alternative explanations must be considered. For example, both variables may result from a common cause and so vary concomitantly.

Correlation Coefficients. Pearson product-moment correlation coefficients were computed between each school characteristic and residuals for grades three, four, and five. Statistical analyses were conducted separately for schools with exceptionally positive and negative residuals. Statistically significant correlations, based on two-tailed significance tests, were found in three instances.

The correlation between staff cost per pupil and the positive residuals for grade four was .57; $p < .01$. This correlation means that as staff cost per pupil increased, positive grade four residuals also tended to increase. Also, the correlation between pupil-teacher ratio and the positive residuals for grade four was $-.53$; $p < .01$. In effect, as pupil-teacher ratios increased, these positive residuals tended to decrease. In a complementary manner, the correlation between pupil-teacher ratio and the negative residuals for grade five was .40; $p < .05$. Thus, as pupil-teacher ratios increased, these negative residuals showed a tendency to increase.

The value of the squared correlation coefficient for any school characteristic and residual is a measure of the strength of the relationship between that variable and the residual. It indicates the percentage of variance of the residual accounted for by the school characteristic.

For example, the value of the squared correlation coefficient for staff cost per pupil and positive residuals for grade four is .325, which is $(.57)^2$. In other words, staff cost per pupil and positive residuals for grade four share 32.5 percent of their variance.

Similarly, the value of the squared correlation coefficient for pupil-teacher ratio and positive residuals for grade four is .281, which is $(-.53)^2$. In effect, pupil-teacher ratio and positive residuals for grade four share 28.1 percent of their variance.

Multiple Regression Analysis. In the previous section, the extent of the relationship between residuals and each school characteristic considered separately was demonstrated. The following section discusses multiple regression techniques, which examine relationships between residuals and school characteristics studied in various combinations. Such techniques may serve as first approximations for predicting and, to some extent, for explaining the relationships between the predictor and criterion variables.

For illustrative purposes, a stepwise multiple regression analysis was calculated on the positive residuals for grade four. Entry levels were selected to enter the school characteristics into the regression equation in hierarchical order. Specifically, the school characteristic that explained the greatest amount of variance together with the one already entered was entered second, and so forth (for further discussion, see Nie and others, 1975, p. 345). The following equation resulted from the regression of school characteristics on the positive residuals of grade four: $Y'_4 = -.055X_a - .607X_b - .350X_c - .682X_d$, where Y'_4 is the predicted residual, X_a is staff cost per pupil, X_b is student attendance, X_c is average daily register and X_d is pupil-teacher ratio. The numerals or constants in the above equation are standardized regression coefficients or beta weights. (See Nie and others, 1975, p. 325, for a distinction between unstandardized and standardized regression coefficients.)

Such equations can be useful for demonstrating relationships between school progress indices and organizational variables. In the above equation, for example, staff cost per pupil, the variable that enters first, has the highest simple correlation (that is, .567) with the positive residuals for grade four. When the second variable, student attendance, enters the analysis, the multiple correlation increases to .657. (See Kerlinger and Pedhazur, 1973, p. 70, for an explanation of a F-test to test the significance of the increment due to variables added to the regression equation.) In other words, staff cost per pupil and student attendance together explain 43.2 percent (that is, the squared multiple correlation) of the variance in positive residuals for grade four. Neither school characteristic alone is able to account for this much of the residual's variability. With the addition of the third variable, average daily register, the multiple correlation increases to .690. When all four variables are considered together, they correlate .746 with the positive residuals for grade four and explain 55.7 percent of the variance in the residuals.

In addition to providing a multiple regression coefficient summarizing the relationship between several independent variables and a dependent variable, multiple regression analysis also takes into account interdependencies of the independent variables. For instance, in the example under consideration, pupil-teacher ratio has a simple correlation of -.526 with the positive residuals for grade four. Therefore, it might be expected to be a better predictor of the residuals than would either student attendance or average daily register, which correlate -.362 and -.028, respectively, with the residuals. In the stepwise analysis, however, both student attendance and average daily register enter the regression equation before pupil-teacher ratio does. Evidently, both student attendance and average daily register, despite lower simple correlations with positive grade four residuals, explain a greater amount of the residual's variance that is unexplained by the variable already in the equation (that is, staff cost per pupil) than does pupil-teacher ratio.

Multiple regression analyses in which the order of variable entry into the regression equation is specified in advance may also be conducted. This is in accordance with Kerlinger and Pedhazur's (1973, p. 49) statement that variables should be entered into regression equations "at the dictates of theory and reasonable interpretation of empirical research findings." It is noted, also, that school characteristics are likely to be correlated with each other. Consequently, an understanding of their impact on student achievement requires analysis of each variable's unique contribution and of the contribution it shares with other variables. Multiple regression techniques may result in this understanding.

School Indices for Successive Years

To what extent is it likely that a school that receives an exceptional index one year will receive an exceptional index the following year? The following section first discusses the relationship between residuals for three consecutive years for all schools. Then it identifies the number of schools with exceptional indices for more than one year.

It should be noted that Brager (1976) cautions that extreme residuals may be statistical artifacts in that they might be due to errors of measurement rather than due to factors of any educational significance. It may be worthwhile, therefore, to consider schools as "exceptional" only if they are consistently distant from the mean for several years (see also Klitgaard and Hall, 1973, pp. 12–13).

Relationship Among Residuals for Consecutive Years. As the same cohort progresses longitudinally up the grades, consecutive residuals appear to be negatively correlated. For example, the residuals obtained for 603 schools for both grade three in 1976 and grade four in 1977 have a correlation of –.094. Similarly, the residuals obtained for 598 schools for both grade four in 1977 and grade five in 1978 have a correlation of –.276. In contrast, when there was a two-year interval, the residuals obtained for both grade three in 1976 and grade five in 1978 have a correlation of .391.

When a residual is exceptional one year, it becomes more difficult for the residual for the same grade in the following year to be exceptional. This is because the exceptional performance or criterion of the first year becomes an exceptionally positive or negative base line or predictor for the succeeding analysis. In addition, residual scores include errors of measurement. If such errors of measurement of residual scores vary markedly one year, theoretically, they are not likely to vary to the same extent the next year. As a result, exceptionally positive or negative residuals are likely to regress towards the mean.

As indicated in Table 3, a pattern of relationships similar to that found for the longitudinal cohort exists for the correlation between residuals for the same grade from one year to the next. The distinction between this and the previous set of correlations is that the cohort analyses involve most of the same children going from one grade to the next in consecutive years. In contrast, the correlations in Table 3 are between the same grade from one year to the next and involve different students, with the exception of a minimal number of holdovers. One may speculate that dynamics similar to the regression-to-the-mean effect discussed previously regarding the longitudinal cohort may be responsible for the pattern of correlation coefficients in Table 3. The number of schools included in each correlation coefficient of Table 3 is indicated in parentheses below the corresponding correlation.

Schools Found Exceptional for More Than One Year. Despite the pattern of negative correlations among residuals for consecutive years, some schools do obtain exceptional indices over consecutive years. Schools with exceptional indices were identified by examining 1976, 1977, and 1978 regression analyses for grades three, four, and five. In total, nine regression analyses were calculated for the three one-year intervals for 1976 through 1978 and for the three grades.

Some grades in some schools manifested exceptional residuals for all three years. Specifically, there were twenty-three instances of positive indices for all three years. There were sixteen schools with positive indices in grade three for three consecutive years. Similarly, there were seven schools which had positive indices for grade five for three consecutive years.

Table 3. Relationship Between Residuals
for the Same Grade in Successive Years

Year	Grade Three 1977	Grade Three 1978	Grade Four 1977	Grade Four 1978	Grade Five 1977	Grade Five 1978
1976	-.089	.366	-.013	.264	-.066	.379
	(609)	(605)	(605)	(600)	(599)	(594)
1977		-.192		-.280		-.247
		(611)		(607)		(605)

Seventeen schools were identified as manifesting exceptionally negative indices for all three years. Specifically, twelve, three, and two schools had negative indices for three consecutive years in grades three, four, and five, respectively.

It was possible, also, to identify several schools with exceptionally positive or negative indices in a given grade for two of the three regression analyses for which data were available. The following combinations of 1978, 1977, and 1976 analyses were examined two at a time: 1978–1977 and 1978–1976. For the 1978–1977 combination, thirty positive and twenty-three negative exceptional residuals were found for all three grades. Similarly, for the 1978–1976 combination, thirty-three positive and thirty-three exceptional residuals were found.

Conclusion

This chapter has outlined and illustrated a set of techniques to identify schools that made greater or less progress than expected. In general, regression techniques have been used to provide preliminary indicators that were used subsequently to classify schools for further analyses. As indicated, there are other ways of generating regression equations, and other types of school indices can be obtained. The particular choice of procedures depends upon various theoretical and methodological considerations.

Administrators must recognize that these techniques make it difficult for a grade to achieve exceptional status for two years in a row as a result of the regression-towards-the-mean effect discussed earlier. Therefore, grades that do achieve such a status for two years or more certainly deserve further examination.

Criterion-referenced tests designed to assess mastery of specific material would be most appropriate to measure school progress. The standardized reading tests that provided the data used in this chapter were norm-referenced tests. Such instruments are designed to achieve maximum discrimination between individuals. In effect, these tests provide scores that indicate the performance of an individual in comparison to the performance of others. As such, the appropriateness of norm-referenced tests to measure school progress is questionable.

It is important to note, also, that regression techniques require at least two sets of test scores. When different standardized tests are used, the content specifications of the tests must be examined to be certain the resulting indices are properly interpreted.

In addition, the criterion of school progress employed in this chapter was reading comprehension. It is important to note, however, that there are other equally important criteria which should be considered. These include, for example, attendance, mathematics achievement, attitudes, communication skills, emotional adjustments, motivation to achieve, and social awareness.

It is apparent that the techniques outlined in this chapter can provide some insight into the nature of exceptional schools. In fact, these statistical techniques may be used to examine the relationship between school progress and many of the variables specified by Gormly in this volume. As indicated earlier, such factors as staff cost per pupil, pupil-teacher ratio, average daily register, student attendance, and student departures distinguish between schools with positive and negative indices. For example, schools characterized by exceptionally negative residuals have lower student attendance, more student departures, and higher average daily registers than schools characterized by exceptionally positive residuals. These findings suggest areas in which greater research attention could be directed in order to determine if changes would result in enhanced school progress.

In conclusion, the methods outlined in this chapter allow school administrators to formulate hypotheses about the potential effects of critical organizational variables on the progress of schools. If subsequent experimental analysis confirms these hypotheses, administrators could begin to change school policies to improve school progress.

References

Armor, D. J. "School and Family Effects on Black and White Achievement: A Re-examination of the USOE Data." In F. Mosteller and D. P. Moynihan (Eds.), *On Equality of Educational Opportunity*. New York: Random House, 1972.

Astin, A. W. "Productivity of Undergraduate Institutions." *Science*, 1962, *136*, 129–135.

Astin, A. W. "Undergraduate Achievement and Institutional Excellence." *Science*, 1968, *161*, 661–668.

Averch, H. A., Carroll, S. J., Donaldson, T. S., Kiesling, H. J., and Pincus, J. *How Effective is Schooling? A Critical Review and Synthesis of Research Findings*. Santa Monica, Calif.: Rand, 1972.

Barnett, V., and Lewis, T. *Outliers in Statistical Data*. New York: Wiley, 1978.

Brager, G. L. "Outliers and Accountability: Fact or Fiction?" Paper presented at

American Educational Research Association annual meeting, San Francisco, California, 1976. (ERIC Document Reproduction Service No. ED 120 230).

Brookover, W. B., and Lezotte, L. W. *Changes in School Characteristics Coincident with Changes in Student Achievement.* East Lansing, Mich.: College of Urban Development of Michigan State University and the Michigan Department of Education, 1977.

Bryant, E. C., Glaser, E., Hansen, M. H., and Kirsch, A. *Association Between Educational Outcomes and Background Variables: A Review of Selected Literature.* Denver: National Assessment of Educational Progress, 1974.

Burstein, L. "Three Key Topics in Regression-Based Analyses of Multilevel Data from Quasi-Experiments and Field Studies." Paper presented at Institute for Research on Teaching, Michigan State University, East Lansing, Mich., 1977.

Burstein, L., and Miller, M. D. "Alternative Analytic Models for Identifying Educational Effects: Where Are We?" Paper presented at American Educational Research Association annual meeting, Toronto, Canada, 1978.

Coleman, H. S., Campbell, E. Q., Hobson, C. J., McPartland, J., Mood, A. M. Weinfeld, F. D., and York, R. L. *Equality of Educational Opportunity.* Washington, D.C.: United States Government Printing Office, 1966.

Convey, J. J. "A Validation of Three Models for Producing School Effectiveness Indices." Paper presented at American Educational Research Association annual meeting, Washington, D.C., 1975.

Convey, J. J. "Determining School Effectiveness Following a Regression Analysis." *Journal of Educational Statistics,* 1977, *2,* 27–39.

Cronbach, L. J. *Essentials of Psychological Testing.* (3rd ed.) New York: Harper & Row, 1970.

Draper, N. R., and Smith, H. *Applied Regression Analysis.* New York: Wiley, 1966.

Dyer, H. S. "Toward Objective Criteria of Professional Accountability in the Schools of New York City." *Phi Delta Kappan,* 1971, *52,* 206–211.

Dyer, H. S., Linn, R. L., and Patton, M. J. "A Comparison of Four Methods of Obtaining Discrepancy Measures Based on Observed and Predicted School System Means on Achievement Tests." *American Educational Research Journal,* 1969, *6,* 591–605.

Edmonds, R. R., and Frederiksen, J. R. *Search for Effective Schools: The Identification and Analysis of City Schools That Are Instructionally Effective for Poor Children.* (Cambridge, Mass.: Center for Urban Studies, Harvard University, 1978.

Hanushek, E. A., and Kain, J. F. "On the Value of Equality of Educational Opportunity as a Guide to Public Policy." In F. Mosteller and D. P. Moynihan (Eds.), *On Equality of Educational Opportunity.* New York: Random House, 1972.

Jencks, C., Smith, M., Acland, M.J.B., Cohen, D., Gintis, H., Heyna, B., and Michelson, S. *Inequality: A Reassessment of the Effect of Family and Schooling in America.* New York: Basic Books, 1972.

Kerlinger, F. N., and Pedhazur, E. J. *Multiple Regression in Behavioral Research.* New York: Holt, Rinehart and Winston, 1973.

Klepak, D. *School Factors Influencing Reading Achievement: A Case Study of Two Inner City Schools.* Albany: Office of Education Performance Review, State of New York, 1974.

Klitgaard, R., and Hall, G. R. *A Statistical Search for Unusually Effective Schools.* Santa Monica, Calif.: Rand, 1973.

McDonald, F. J., Forehand, G. A., Marco, G. L., Murphy, R. T., and Quirk, T. J. *A Design for an Accountability System for the New York City School System.* Princeton, N.J.: Educational Testing Service, 1972.

Marco, G. L. "A Comparison of Selected School Effective Measures Based on Longitudinal Data." *Journal of Educational Measurement*, 1974, 2, 225–231.

Mayeske, G. W., Wisler, C. E., Beaton, A. E., Weinfeld, F. D., Cohen, W. M., Okada, T., Proshek, J. M., and Tabler, K. A. *A Study of Our Nation's Schools.* Washington, D.C.: U.S. Government Printing Office, 1972.

Mosteller, F., and Moynihan, D. P. (Eds.). *On Equality of Educational Opportunity.* New York: Random House, 1972.

Nie, N., Hull, C. H., Jenkins, J. G., Steinbrenner, K., and Bent, D. H. *Statistical Package for the Social Sciences.* (2nd ed.) New York: McGraw-Hill, 1975.

Pedhazur, E. J. "Analytic Methods in Studies of Educational Effects." In F. N. Kerlinger (Ed.), *Review of Research in Education.* Vol. 3. Itasca, Ill.: Peacock, 1975.

Rutter, M., Maughan, B., Morimore, P., Ouston, J., and Smith, A. *Fifteen Thousand Hours.* Cambridge, Mass.: Harvard University Press, 1979.

School Profiles 1976–1977. New York: Board of Education of the City of New York, 1978.

Sewell, W. H., Hauser, R. M., and Featherman, D. *Schooling and Achievement in American Society.* New York: Academic Press, 1976.

Smith, M. S. "Equality of Educational Opportunity: The Basic Findings Reconsidered." In F. Mosteller and D. P. Moynihan (Eds.), *On Equality of Educational Opportunity.* New York: Random House, 1972.

Spady, W. G. "The Impact of School Resources on Students." In F. N. Kerlinger (Ed.), *Review of Research in Education.* Vol. 1. Itasca, Ill.: Peacock, 1973.

Summers, A. A., and Wolfe, B. L. *Which School Resources Help Learning? Efficiency and Equity in Philadelphia Public Schools.* Philadelphia: Federal Reserve Bank of Philadelphia, 1975.

United States Department of Health, Education, and Welfare. *A Practical Guide to Measuring Project Impact on Student Achievement.* Washington, D.C., 1975.

University of the State of New York. *Variables Related to Student Performance and Resource Allocation Decisions at the School District Level.* Albany, N.Y.: State Education Department, Bureau of School Programs Evaluation, 1972.

University of the State of New York. *What Research Says About Improving Student Performance: A Manual for Administrators.* Albany, N.Y.: State Education Department, Bureau of School Programs Evaluation, 1973.

University of the State of New York. *Which School Factors Relate to Learning? Summary of Findings of Three Sets of Studies.* Albany, N.Y.: State Education Department, Bureau of School Programs Evaluation, 1976.

Gary M. Kippel is the assistant director of educational research at the New York City Board of Education. In addition he is an adjunct associate professor, Pace University and New York University.

*The editor finds consensus on ten points among the
authors of this book. The ten points form the basis of
some recommendations for those conducting studies
that measure effectiveness.*

Summary: Developing a
Successful Measurement
Program

Dan Baugher

The next decade will see an ever-increasing emphasis upon accountability
(Windle, 1979). This emphasis will not be on a limited set of operations.
Rather, it appears that evaluations of effectiveness will be conducted in a
variety of settings. The previous chapters in this volume emphasize the
diversity of the settings in which questions of efficacy can appear. Yet they
are not the only settings. For example, the evaluation of psychopharmacotherapeutic agents is not the only area of concern to evaluators of
psychological therapies. Assessments of other strategies of therapeutic
intervention, such as behavioral therapy, are also of growing concern to
government sponsors (Barlow, 1980).

Nonetheless, it seems safe to say that the authors of these sourcebook
chapters show consensus on a variety of issues. This concluding chapter
summarizes ten areas of general agreement. While other areas of agreement
may be found and debates over the relative importance of these ten areas
might arise, they still reflect important areas for implementors of evaluation strategies to consider before beginning their measurement programs.

No Single Model of Effectiveness. What constitutes effectiveness is a
matter of individual perspective. There is a great deal of subjectivity in our

D. Baugher (Ed.). *New Directions for Program Evaluation: Measuring Effectiveness*, no. 11.
San Francisco: Jossey-Bass, September 1981

determination of what makes an individual, program, or organization effective. Economic, social, psychological, moral, and legal dimensions permeate our views of effectiveness and, in many instances, effectiveness on one of these dimensions may lead to ineffectiveness on another dimension. As such, there is often no single model for defining effectiveness in any given situation. This is not to say that the investigator should not focus on a particular type of effectiveness. The point to keep in mind is that an operation can look effective from one perspective and ineffective from another perspective. Ultimately, *the investigator should determine which type of effectiveness is of the greatest concern to the constituency or constituencies to which he or she must report.*

Need for Multiple Indicators of Efficacy. There is no single measure or composite measure of efficacy possible in most situations. Summarizing across a variety of different measures may actually obscure important results. In addition, investigators may find themselves dealing with multiple constituencies. Each of these constituencies may have very different views of what constitutes success in the area of interest. As a result, *investigators should attempt to devise a measurement system that taps as many different measures of effectiveness as possible in the situation under investigation.* Measures selected for evaluating the efficacy of a particular domain of activity should reflect the dimensionality of the situation as it truly exists. Subjective as well as objective measures of success may need to be used. Personal opinions of those involved with the activity may be a useful source of information and should not be eliminated from consideration simply because they are too subjective or hard to measure.

Emphasizing the Importance of Effectiveness Measurement. It is not uncommon for investigators to run into considerable misunderstanding of and indifference toward their efforts to assess effectiveness. In some instances, those working in the area of interest may never have had such an assessment before and may not understand why "now" is the time for an assessment of their endeavors. Yet their assistance and understanding is often critical to the success of an effectiveness measurement program. If workers in the domain of interest do not understand the need for the specific measurements taken, they may cause unreliable or invalid data to be collected. For this reason, *investigators must make every effort to persuade those working in the area of interest that the resulting information is important to the long-term survival of the organization for which they are working.*

Focusing on Solutions to Problems, Not Past Mistakes. Even if those engaged in the activity under examination are persuaded of the importance of the measurements taken, they may still be quite worried about the consequences the investigation will have on them. It is only human to be anxious about evaluation of one's efforts. Such anxiety over evaluation can cause many problems, including falsification of data or general resistance to the investigation. Yet if the activity was worth evaluating in the first place, a negative evaluation should not automatically lead to suspended activity. Rather, such an outcome should lead to changes that enable those involved in the activity to perform their jobs more effectively. In short, *the goal of an effectiveness measurement program should be to provide solutions to problems when problems exist. If no problems are apparent at the end of the investigation, praise should be directed toward those responsible for success of the activity under question.* Ultimately, evaluations that focus on past mistakes are likely to be counterproductive because they lead to defensiveness as opposed to amelioration of problems.

Planning for Evaluation. All too frequently, evaluation is conducted as a *post hoc* enterprise. At some point someone determines that it is time to evaluate a particular activity. Unfortunately, this approach makes it very difficult to evaluate the activity at all. Important data often are not collected or, if they are collected, inappropriate tools of questionable reliability or validity are used. This approach to evaluation is difficult to defend. Evaluation of an activity must become an integral part of the planning process. *When planning is conducted regarding the goals of the activity and methods to accomplish those goals, methods of evaluation should also be considered.* In this way, more comprehensive evaluations can be conducted and more valid information can be obtained.

Evaluation as an Ongoing Process. In many cases, evaluation is a one-shot deal. Someone is called in to make the evaluation, a report is produced, and evaluation of the activity is concluded. This limited approach is not very satisfactory. It does not lead to a continual refinement of the activity. Quite often such an approach leads to nothing. The report is filed and the evaluation is considered "done." As such, *it is essential that evaluation be an ongoing part of an activity when possible.* As multiple evaluations are undertaken, those involved in the activity may be persuaded of the importance of evaluation. As a result, changes in the activity are more likely to be initiated. In addition, such an ongoing process can lead to refinement of the evaluation process itself and to more valid conclusions.

Accurate Documentation of the Evaluation Process. The final product of any evaluation study is information. Consequently, *it is important that the methods used to develop this information and the raw data upon which the information was based be thoroughly documented and available.* The rationale for this is obvious. At times, the results of an evaluation effort can have serious consequences. Since methods of data collection and the data themselves are critical to making valid inferences about the efficacy of a given activity, this information should be available to other investigators who may question the conclusions found in a particular study. Unfortunately, effectiveness measurement is not an exact science. In many cases, alternative hypotheses may be postulated, or critical biases caused by the methods of investigation may exist. Sometimes these problems may slip the attention of a particular investigator and reanalysis of the data may be in order. In other cases, accurate procedural documentation of one study is important to a similar study in another setting. Without such documentation, comparability across studies would be almost impossible (as is often the case now).

Using Appropriate Methodological Approaches. Problems of measurement, design, and statistical interpretation confront all evaluators of effectiveness. Ultimately, *it is best to use familiar, well-documented procedures to determine the likelihood of changes having occurred due to chance fluctuations.* The nature of the methodological problems confronting investigators will vary from situation to situation. In choosing a statistical technique, evaluators are wise to select the simplest technique possible for the situation. Selection of overly complex techniques when simpler approaches are available may be counterproductive, since the users of the information may not be able to understand the techniques. In addition, novel techniques may reduce the likelihood that the study will be replicated. It is obvious that the use of a complex statistical analysis cannot make up for a poor research design. In the final analysis, it is the goal of the investigator to determine the probability that the activity under investigation caused the particular outcome. This determination can be accomplished only by eliminating as many rival hypotheses for explaining the outcome as possible (that is, achieving internal validity). In those instances where generalizability of the results is also important, the investigator will have to be concerned with the representativeness of the situation (that is, external validity) as well.

Careful Communication of Evaluation Information. Evaluation studies are generally conducted to aid in the process of deciding how a particular activity is to be conducted. For this reason, investigators should be very careful in communicating their results to decision makers. Some very recent research on this issue suggests that negative findings have a greater weight than positive information (Locatis and others, 1980). Managers may overreact to negative information but discount positive information. In fact, neutral information may be perceived in a negative light (Locatis and others, 1980). Fortunately, administrators who are familiar with the evaluation procedures seem less likely to overreact to the information. As such, *a full, understandable description of the study must be written so that a minimal misuse of the evaluation information will occur.*

Need for Replication Studies. While it is true that some evaluation studies are concerned with a single problem in a very specific situation, many others are concerned with broader issues. Concerns over what training procedures, therapeutic approaches, performance evaluation techniques, and educational approaches are most effective are examples of areas in which replications would be most useful. For this reason, *evaluators should make every effort to replicate their results in the same or different settings.* While classical scientific replications are seldom possible in the kinds of program settings with which evaluators are concerned, efforts can certainly be made to apply the same measurement techniques, observation schedules, and so on. When it is apparent that evaluators are studying a phenomenon with far-reaching implications. replication becomes more important. However, replication of results within even a narrow area of concern will add greater strength to the conclusions. In general, the more often a particular result is replicated the more confidence one can have regarding the outcome.

This chapter has outlined ten areas of agreement among the contributors to this sourcebook. Each of these areas takes the form of a recommendation. Yet, a review of them suggests that none are really new. It is unfortunate that such a restatement of critical recommendations is judged necessary, but many effectiveness studies have failed to take into consideration certain of these points. Now is the time for the field of effectiveness measurement to start taking its own recommendations seriously. Solid, well-designed effectiveness studies are needed. While it is often difficult to do research in "real-life" settings, it is not impossible.

References

Barlow, David H. (Ed.). *Behavioral Assessment of Adult Disorders.* New York: Guilford Press, 1980.

Locatis, C. N., Smith, J. K., and Blake, V. L. "Effects of Evaluation Information on Decisions." *Evaluation Review,* 1980, *4* (6), 809–823.

Windle, C. "Developmental Trends in Program Evaluation." *Evaluation and Program Planning,* 1979, *2* (3), 193–196.

Dan Baughers is an associate professor in the Lubin Schools of Business Administration of management, Pace University, New York City. He is interested in the prediction of socially relevant criteria, such as employee effectiveness, through an examination of individual differences. He has worked as a consultant on problems of measurement and prediction for AT&T and Hardee's Food Systems, Inc.

Index